Reading
and
Successful
Living

Reading
and
Successful
Living

THE FAMILY-SCHOOL PARTNERSHIP

Edited by

Lester Asheim
D. Philip Baker
Virginia H. Mathews

with a Foreword by
Mrs. George Bush

Library Professional Publications
1983

First published in 1983 as a Library Professional Publication,
an imprint of The Shoe String Press, Inc.,
Hamden, Connecticut 06514

Printed in the United States of America

Library of Congress Cataloging in Publication Data

Main entry under title:

Reading and successful living.

  Papers originally presented at the Reading and
Successful Living Symposium Nov. 1981, held under the
auspices of the Center for the Book at Library of
Congress.
    1. Books and reading—United States—Congresses.
2. Libraries and families—United States—Congresses.
3. Libraries and schools—Congresses. I. Asheim,
Lester Eugene, 1914–   . II. Baker, D. Philip,
1937–   . III. Mathews, Virginia H. IV. Reading
and Successful Living Symposium   (1981 : Library of
Congress) V. Center for the Book.
Z1003.2.R4   1983   028′.9   82-24973
ISBN 0-208-02004-7 (pbk.)

To all who feel an obligation to
give to every child a vision of the
successful life, an idea of all the
kinds of success a life may hold,
and the wherewithal through
books to broaden and pursue
that vision, this book is dedicated.

Contents

Foreword

(Originally presented at the luncheon during the Reading and Successful Living Symposium on Thursday, November 19, 1981, this talk by Mrs. George Bush, wife of the Vice President of the United States, provides, we believe, a graceful and lively foreword to this book. Barbara Bush was introduced on this occasion by Daniel J. Boorstin, the Librarian of Congress, who called her "an apostle of literacy in the most visible place in the world. We applaud Mrs. Bush's leadership," said Dr. Boorstin, "and we look forward to the continuing exercise of her energy, her intelligence, and her imagination in making us the most reading nation in the world.")

I am delighted to be here at this center for books and to be taking a small part in this prestigious national symposium on "Reading and Successful Living: The Family-School Partnership." I know that I can't outexpert the experts, and I am not going to try. Instead, I thought I might tell you how I chose my projects and what I am doing.

When it became clear to me that George was really going to seek the presidency, and knowing that a First Lady has a wonderful opportunity to help others, I started thinking about a project for myself. First, I set the ground rules: my project must not become commercial, for the next president of the United States was going to have enough trouble without having a wife who added to his burdens; it must not depend on government money—the next president was going to have to cut federal spending; and it should help as many Americans as possible. I thought about all of the things that interested me and all of the things that worried me: the economy, unemployment, inner cities, welfare mothers locked into poverty, traffic, pollution, the aging, rapid transit (and the lack thereof), drug abuse, the women's movement, hospital work (I've always worked in hospitals), and crime in the streets. Suddenly, it became obvious to me that I should get interested in none of these for my project, but should throw all of my energies into helping to wipe out illiteracy.

All of these problems that worry me would be helped if more people could read. For instance, there are eight million people who are unemployed, and yet *The Wall Street Journal* tells us that employers cannot find enough applicants who are sufficiently skilled in basic reading, writing, and math to fill empty positions. Also, there is a *direct* correlation between crime and illiteracy. The California Youth Authority reports that 50 percent of their inmates are functional illiterates—that is, they read below the sixth-grade level. Florida Judge Charles Phillips reports that 80 percent of the new criminals passing before his bench would not be there if they had graduated from high school and could read and write. I could go on—but that would be a little like telling Noah about the flood!

Well, George didn't become president, but it turns out that the vice president's wife can also raise a crowd—and here you are! So I am spending my time visiting schools, libraries, churches, service groups, clinics, colleges, and community centers, encouraging reading, the teaching of reading, the necessity of reading, and the joys of reading. I am also encouraging the giving of time and money by individuals and corporations toward the fight against illiteracy. As is always the case, I have gained much more than I have given. I have seen a legally blind man in Boston teach two children to read. He says to them: "How do I know what it says? I can't see. Spell it, sound it out." And they do, and the joy he gets and they get is so exciting.

I have seen a school in Philadelphia run by a tiny staff of three nuns, and parents, many of them on welfare, but the parents know the importance of an education, and rush twice a month with their twenty-five dollars to pay the tuition. They know that an education is the key that unlocks the door to the American dream, and that no sacrifice is too big. I have seen the parents at the Briargrove Elementary School in Houston—at the exact other end of the spectrum, economically—working as teachers' aides, and so thrilled with the dramatic rise in the test results. I have seen a kindergarden teacher at the Webb School in the District teach five-year-olds. Watching her was like watching an athletic event: the energy she put into her teaching was an inspiration. Thank heavens we are bonding parents and schools again!

In Boston alone there are 3,000 volunteers in fifty schools, and they could use twice that many. It was there that I saw a wonderfully stylish lady teaching French in a volunteer capacity. She pulled the most extraordinary things out of her pocketbook and then she said the word for each one in French, and the children would copy her. I was told that she had done this for years and that she was a very effective teacher. Adele Rogers, the wife of the former secretary of state, William Rogers, has tutored two days a week for the past ten years; one day in the District schools, the other in the New York City public schools. James Hunt, the governor of North Carolina, and his wife, volunteer in the public schools one morning a week. And this is just a small representation of the wonderful people I have seen.

Many corporations are helping, committing their employees to several hours a week on company time. I visited with one lady who was on loan from Prudential Insurance Co. She said that the most wonderful part of the program was that now she knew how to help her own children at home. In New York City, where 15,000 volunteers help in 544 schools, I met a group that helped Cambodian children to speak and read English. One elderly lady told me that she had been desperately lonely until she volunteered, and her face lit up as she told me that she had never been lonely since. I have visited schools in Baltimore, New York, Houston, Philadelphia, Milwaukee, the District of Columbia, and San Antonio, Texas. I have been very much impressed with the volunteerism from every sector, but even more than that, with the superintendents, the principals, the teachers, and librarians. I am struck by the dedication of these wonderful people, who work in hot, crowded classrooms for less material satisfactions than most, doing their own jobs and sometimes ours. I have learned that one person can make a difference. Just look at Margaret McNamara and the job she did—starting as one woman in one Washington, D.C. public school. Today there are over 100,000 volunteers in the Reading is Fundamental (RIF) program—nearly 40 percent of them parents. What a joy these book distributions have been for me! Someone else (usually a lot of someone elses) does a lot of work selecting the books, setting up the program and arranging the day; I come in on the big day and help to distribute the books. Wonderful! Right here in the Stevens School we met an extraordinary reading specialist who told her second-grade class a very scary Halloween story before the book distribution. For me, that was the icing on the cake. This past Thursday in San Antonio, Texas, I went to the

Smith Elementary School for a RIF distribution, and the students sang a great song written by their resident poet. The chorus was: "I need to read, I re–a–lly need to read!" I wish you could have seen those children choosing their own books! And look at Mardy Van Arsdale in upstate New York: she read about Project Read, a program started in Idaho, and she started it in Wyoming County, New York. She worked with every known group—schools, libraries, men's clubs, community centers—any group that would listen. She flooded the county with bumper stickers, posters, and word of mouth, saying, "Have You Read to Your Child 15 Minutes Today?" She got the children and teachers on her side, and they worked on the parents. They found the reading interest was way up, and as an added bonus, the time spent side by side with their children did wonders for family relationships. One lady had an idea.

I couldn't be in this great library without mentioning my trips to two other great libraries: the Enoch Pratt Library in Baltimore, and the New York Public Library. Both of these wonderful institutions do a great job with adult illiteracy. Their programs have helped people to do such things as enter a high school equivalency program, obtain a job, get a driver's license, read bedtime stories to their children, read the Bible, and write letters to their friends and loved ones—tasks they had never been able to do before.

I have read with great interest the three purposes of this symposium. I am not qualified to recommend priorities in national educational policies relating to reading, nor am I qualified to help the four sponsoring organizations to shape their goals and programs for the immediate future. But as an enthusiastic cheerleader, I can help focus national attention on the essential role of an active, two-way family partnership in encouraging reading. I am more than willing to help, whether it be RIF, Laubach International, The International Reading Association, National Volunteers in Public Schools, Volunteers in Public Schools, Reading Olympics, Project Read, Parent-Teacher Associations (PTAs), libraries, or projects having to do with children with learning disabilities.

Please call on me when you need me. The job is immense, and when I get discouraged by the enormity of the problem of 23 million known illiterates in this country, I remember that remarkable Helen Keller, who said that literature kept her from being disenfranchized from life. Deaf and blind, Helen Keller could read. Somebody taught *her* to read. If Helen Keller could read, surely we can teach many of these hearing and sighted 23 million Americans to read. I congratulate you all on your chosen professions. As a Johnny-come-very-lately, I am your greatest advocate and cheerleader.

BARBARA BUSH

Preface

This book, with its formal background papers, its responses and discussions, and its recommendations, is the product of a symposium held under the auspices, and with the support of, the Center for the Book in the Library of Congress. It took place on the evening of November 18, and the following day, November 19, 1981, at the Library of Congress's Madison Building in Washington, D.C.

The idea that the Center should devote one of its forums to problems and opportunities relating to the use of books and reading in the schools was suggested several times during the annual meeting of the Center's Advisory Board in 1980. It was developed into the concept of a jointly sponsored and planned symposium, involving four of the major educational organizations most directly concerned with children and reading. These were: the American Association of School Administrators, the American Association of School Librarians (a division of the American Library Association), the International Reading Association, and the National Congress of Parents and Teachers. The process was begun by Center for the Book Advisory Board members Lester Asheim (ALA), D. Philip Baker (AASL), Virginia H. Mathews (AASL and IRA), and Ralph Staiger (IRA). They were joined by William Spadey, Associate Director of AASA and members of his board, and Alice Troy, staff member of NCPT, and members of the NCPT board.

This group met several times in Washington, D.C. to work out a philosophy and a structure for the symposium that would interest and engage members of the organizations; to choose writers for the four background papers that would lay the basis for discussion; and to select opening night and luncheon speakers, the respondents, and participants.

Three purposes for the enterprise were identified: (1) to recommend priorities in national educational policy relating to reading; (2) to focus attention on the essential role of an active two-way family-school partnership in encouraging reading as a lifetime habit; and (3) to help the four sponsoring organizations to shape their goals and programs in the future.

It was decided that this was to be an invitational event, with space for about sixty participants. Nearly everyone invited represented more than one area of expertise, and experience, relevant to the subject matter. There was criticism from some people who felt that a group gathered to ponder reading and successful living should not be limited to the "experts." We even had criticisms from one or two people who thought that we should not be talking about reading at all. Their contention was either that (1) reading is an obsolete activity, or (2) reading is an elitist activity. We forged ahead, however, confident that our objectives would best be served by involving some of the most experienced and thoughtful people in the field to make the policy-level recommendations we hoped to produce. We believed also that if reading has been perceived to be an elitist activity in the past, then it is high time that its rewards be shared more widely. We were always aware, however, thanks largely to the quiet warnings of Dr. Asheim—expressed so well in his summary at the end of the symposium day—that the values that color our attitudes toward reading are not universally shared. Freedom to read *does* have its opponents.

Right from the first meeting, it was agreed that the symposium should deal with the achievement of reading abilities that would yield a high level of personal competence, contribution, self-identity and influence, and not just functional literacy, minimum skills, and low-level expectations. Another significant position taken was that of thinking and talking in terms of a total *family*-school partnership, and not just a partnership of parents with the schools. A major consideration was that the symposium would be held at a time when attempts were being made to shift funding of education, in it's entirety, away from the federal to the state and local levels, potentially signalling a retreat from the traditional commitment to education as a national priority.

We identified four elements that we believed undergirded the equation, Reading – Successful Living, sustained by the family-school partnership. These were: *books and other reading materials, instruction, motivation;* and *access*—physical and psychological—to all of these. Four papers were commissioned: they were to be the springboards to discussion. Each paper was to view each of the component elements from different perspec-

xvi

tives: that of a school administrator, a reading teacher, a parent, and a library media specialist. Each writer was to consider all of the elements but was asked to cover in particular depth the one with which he or she had the greatest involvement and responsibility. Thus, Dr. Verne A. Duncan, State Superintendent of Public Instruction in Oregon, addressed the subject from his viewpoint as school administrator, with emphasis on access; Dr. Leo Fay, Chairman of the Reading Education Department at Indiana University and a past president of the International Reading Association, addressed the issues with emphasis on reading instruction. Dr. Edward L. Palmer, vice president for research for the Children's Television Workshop, who has done a great deal of research on motivation and parent reinforcement, in addition to being, in fact, a parent himself emphasized motivation; and Dr. Peggy Sullivan, Dean of the College of Professional Studies at Northern Illinois University, and a past president of the American Library Association, with experience as both a school and public librarian and educator, addressed the subject with emphasis on materials.

One paper was introduced by its author at each of the four work sessions. Nine respondents, with remarks prepared in advance, led the way to floor discussion. At lunch, the vivacious wife of the Vice President of the United States gave the talk we have reproduced here as the Foreword; on the opening evening, the context or keynote talk—herein reproduced as the Introduction—was given by Dr. Robert Andringa, Executive Director of the Education Commission of the States.

We were reminded of many things by the symposium experience, short though it was. For example, to consider even one facet of need, opportunity, expectation, and cause in education—such as reading and the family-school partnership—one must look at the larger social and economic context; at adult learning, demographics, financial bases, employment, and technology, for instance. Questions must be asked: What do we mean by families? What do people really expect from the schools? Why is there hostility between communities and their school systems, and what can be done about it?

The symposium and its recommendations, presented herein, were developed against a background of certain assumptions/facts, some of which were:

1. The phrase "successful living" implies success of many

kinds: material/economic, self-realization, the ability to appreciate and contribute, and the ability to cope—anything, in short that spells success in individual terms. The concept implied is that reading is a significant factor in shaping success of many kinds as well as shaping values and one's very notion of what constitutes success worth aspiring to and working toward.

2. High levels of reading skill and motivation have a symbolic value as well as an immensely practical one: they spell freedom, independence, growth, choice, power—or at least their potential—for those who have mastered "influential literacy."

3. We have entered a period in which we may see the decrease of advocacy for children's needs. We may also witness a decline in the belief in the paramount importance of education as a national commitment. Within this framework, reading and libraries, which represent free access to information and the skill to use it effectively, appear to be on the downturn.

4. The nature of volunteerism and of volunteers has changed significantly in recent years. Factors at work include women working for pay outside the home, a higher and growing proportion of older people in the population, and a more concrete return expected by volunteers for their investment of time—to name only a few.

5. Family support of reading interests and motivations in the home is not limited to parents alone, but involves grandparents and other extended family members as well as other children in the family. It is a key ingredient in the kind and level of reading that makes possible job flexibility, work satisfaction, entrepreneurship, and creative leisure. Positive reading behavior that is modeled by adults in the home is an important factor in this support.

6. The development of reading motivations and skills, especially the higher order skills of inferential and critical reading/thinking, can be improved through a family-school partnership. There appear to be obstacles to the achievement of this partnership, but they can be overcome when both parents and educators have a genuine interest and a stake in the improvement of reading ability and opportunity, and when they believe that the goal is worth the effort.

7. Parent, teacher, and community expectations about children's reading are key factors in the development of lifetime

reading habits. Teachers, as well as parents and the wider community, must have a positive attitude toward teaching, toward the importance of reading, and toward student potential.

There is increasing emphasis on the necessity of the family-school collaboration, but at present national coordination and leadership is lacking. We now have, we believe, the beginning of a plan for those who are responsible for focusing ideas and spurring action at the school system level, in individual class-rooms and school buildings, in homes, day-care centers, libraries, and many other sites. This includes statewide consortia of educational agencies and organizations, local reading councils, PTAs, school and library media associations, and many other groups with which our communities are so richly endowed. The symposium was taped in its entirety, and remarks by the respondents and participants were transcribed and edited for presentation in book form. Due to the always-present difficulties of recording and transcribing the discussions of a large and lively group, many comments from the floor could not be heard or ascribed, but we have reflected their spirit and as much of their essence as possible.

We offer these recommendations with sincere thanks and appreciation to the many people who made the symposium and this book possible. First, of course, to the staff of the Library of Congress: to Dr. Daniel J. Boorstin, who envisioned the Center for the Book and brought it to life, and to Mrs. Boorstin, who participated in the symposium with such enthusiasm; to Dr. Carol Nemeyer, who watches over all the external and often complex relationships of the Library of Congress and the Center for the Book, and who supported the symposium with such particular interest and care; to John Y. Cole, Executive Director of the Center for the Book during the planning period and who, up until two months or so before the symposium, was our staff supporter and colleague of inestimable value; and to Dr. Judith O'Sullivan who, as executive director, carried on with us right through the symposium and its follow-up—we thank you. We are grateful, too, for the advice and interest of so many members of the Center for the Book's Advisory Board.

We cannot be too glowing in our appreciation of the paper writers; the speakers and respondents; Mrs. George Bush and Robert Andringa, who contributed so much to our thinking and whose ideas will be sent forth in ever-widening circles through this book; and of the participants who read the papers, who listened and thought and cared and expounded. We are also indebted to the staffs and boards and members of the sponsoring organizations, who made lists, planned meetings, and spent so much time and effort on behalf of the symposium.

Finally, there are two individuals to whom a very special thank you is due for arranging additional funding when it was needed to follow through on our commitment to the symposium and its recommendations: Ralph Staiger, Executive Director of the International Reading Association, and Dan Lacy, senior vice president of McGraw Hill, Inc. who is also a member of the executive committee of the Center for the Book. Through their respective good offices, the International Reading Association made a substantial contribution to carrying out both the symposium and this report, and McGraw Hill, Inc. provided the sum that made it possible to prepare this book for publication. We thank both these organizations most sincerely. This whole enterprise, like the Center for the Book itself, whose activities and programs—including this one—are supported by private donations, has been a demonstration of synergism, of private sectors and people cooperating in the public interest. We are happy to share it with you.

Hamden, Connecticut   THE EDITORS
August 1982

PART I
The Symposium

Introduction

(Originally presented as the opening event of the Reading and Successful Living Symposium on Wednesday evening, November 18, 1981 in the Madison Building of the Library of Congress, this talk by Dr. Robert Andringa, transcribed from tape, provides for this book, as it did for the symposium itself, a framework and an introduction for the discussions that follow. Dr. Andringa was introduced by Dr. Carol Nemeyer, Associate Librarian of Congress for National Programs, who noted the following:

Dr. Robert Andringa assumed the position of Executive Director, Education Commission of the States, in September, 1980. ECS is a sixteen-year-old compact of states created to assist state policy makers by undertaking education research, providing clearinghouse functions, sponsoring a variety of forums on policy issues, and representing state education interests to the federal government. Each state has seven commissioners, including the governor, legislative leaders, and other education policy makers. ECS headquarters is in Denver, Colorado.

Dr. Andringa has spent his professional life in education and government service. His three degrees from Michigan State University include a Ph.D in 1967 in higher education administration. He served in the United States Army from 1967–69. In 1969, he joined the staff of former Congressman Al Quie to work on higher education legislation, and was named Minority Staff Director of the House Committee on Education and Labor by Quie in 1971. After managing Quie's successful campaign to become Governor of Minnesota in 1978, Andringa became Director of Policy Research in the Governor's Office, until his appointment to the ECS post.)

As I understand it, this is to be a working conference which challenges you to think as people of action and to act as people of thought. I believe that nothing is meaningful without a context, and I have been asked to put this conference, or its topic, in a context of what is happening in the world today—

especially the political and economic world. As one looks down the road, it is all too easy to be pessimistic, but with a little more effort, we can take an optimistic view of the 1980s and see opportunities for advancing the cause of a learning society. The depression in education has sapped the strength of its leadership too greatly already. But I don't endorse blind optimism.

We are in a period of immense change. What I would like to do is to take a look at some of the dynamics of this change, and then look at a few of the implications for education; and to review briefly the role of government in education, especially the shift in philosophy with the current administration. Dan Yankelovich said recently to a group of educators that in his view we are in one of the most uncertain and unstable times of the past half century. He likened it to going through a process of grief and adjustment to the loss of our position as the number-one society of the world; to the fact that next year may not be as good as this year; and to the knowledge that our national security may not be as secure as we had hoped that it would be.

Some of the elements with which educators and state policy makers are grappling are demographic: we've been adjusting to enrollment declines in elementary and secondary education for several years; post-secondary enrollment is on the verge of a decade of decline in some states that is as large as 30 or 35 percent. This is a national phenomenon, but ranges of data among the states are great. The public is not happy with our schools. We have long assumed a fairly large majority of people who have a real and personal interest in the public schools. Demographic shifts are changing this. In the 1950s, three out of five voters had children in school. In this decade one out of five voters have children in school. The flip side of this set of numbers tells where the public's interest is likely to be: before World War II there were nine people in the work force supporting every one person of age sixty-five or above; today there are only three persons supporting every person of age sixty-five and above. By 1990, the ratio will be two to one. These statistics about our aging population present new opportunities for continuing education for adults. On the other hand, those who predict population upturns tell us to expect within a few years an increase of 25 percent in the population of those age five and below. This indicates a need, in a world of working mothers and single parent families, for day-care and other preschool provi-

4

sions and experiences. The big question here is whether the public schools are going to be able to fill that need, or whether we are going to have to depend upon employers to fill it.

ECONOMICS

Inflation is a major enemy of education. There seems to be little hope that any level of government will be able to increase annual spending to keep up with inflation, and in a labor intensive industry like education, costs run slightly ahead, even, of the consumer index. There will be continuing pressures on the local tax base which supports education. We're at a point where perhaps some major structural changes in the way education is organized might be necessary. Most states are faced with the same extreme financial pressures as is the federal budget. We must recognize that we have many different economies at work in the nation, however, with states like Michigan and Oregon on the downside end of the pole, and states like Louisiana, Texas, and Alaska on the other.

TECHNOLOGY

Any assessment of education must acknowledge the awesome changes that technology is bringing to our lives. The computer companies were pretty smart to introduce video games—there is a whole generation out there at ease with and ready to handle the technology. As we hitch up cable systems to computers and videodiscs, we are going to have a whole new way of learning. Not only can school help children to develop skills; technology is now capable of breaking up the virtual monopoly the schools have had on learning in our society. This is especially true at the post-secondary level, where there is a proven capacity to offer quality learning experience at the convenience of the learner, at the individual's speed, and at considerable savings compared to mounting tuition costs. This capacity will be available to any number of public and private enterprises, not just to schools and colleges. Will the educational community recognize the potential in educational breakthrough, or will we try to argue against depending on technology for any major role in the learning process?

Let's look for a minute at values. Several writers are trying

5

to help us sort out the shift in values. The values of our society underwent a fantastic change in the sixties and seventies. Now we seem to be rejecting some of those values. Quoting directly from Yankelovich's recent speech to a group of educators: "If you take the ethics of the sixties, when you had those who were the recipients of the greatest privileges society offers (upper-middle-class upbringing, education, sensibility) seeking their fulfillment through mountain climbing rather than contributing to the economy and the society, that's a social ethic in which the individual's wants and the society's needs don't fit. What we're struggling with today is a vacuum in a sense. We had a social ethic, a very strong one; the ethic of self-denial, and the rebellion was against that. A handle for the resulting ethic is the handle that Tom Wolfe pinned on it—'the me decade'—and a total concern with self. We now have the discovery that that isn't working too well, partly because of changed conditions, and partly because it doesn't bear up well under experience. We are struggling now to evolve a new social ethic out of the pieces of both the old that seemed to work. From a political point of view, in that kind of climate, we simply have to get some real control over our practical problems and our institutions, of which the education system is one."

Although we are jettisoning some of those values from the sixties and seventies, one of the values that remains strong is the right to choices. Women should have the choice of getting married or not getting married, of working or not working. Students should have the choice of going to college or not going to college. Yankelovich says that according to his research, 73 percent of the population rates this as a value that is very significant to them. This has implications for an era in which interest in tuition tax credits, vouchers, and independent schools is rising, and gives us a reason not to be too quick to say that this is a condemnation of the public schools. It may be in part, but it may also reflect the fundamental value we place on having a choice. Again, the public schools, if they are wise, will understand the importance of this value and provide the choices themselves—within the public school system—or they can offer just one set of options and be prepared to take the consequences.

Finally, in the area of values, I sense a growing interest in spiritual values by people who want to explore the spiritual

6

dimensions of life, who want to express them. Yet schools and colleges seem to be among those institutions most set against intellectually honest religious discussions. Experience shows, I believe, that persons whose faith is alive, real, and personal are among the most effective contributors to society.

The federal share of educational funding has been about 8 percent for the last few years. However, there are wide variations, so that some areas might be getting upwards of 20 or even 30 percent. We now have an administration which wants to reverse this support and lessen the regulation of schools. This view seems to reflect the majority opinion, and there seems to be considerable support for this philosophy among governors and state legislators. For example, at the National Governors' Association conference last summer, the association's committee on education, taking a reading on the climate of the times, drafted a more limited definition of the federal role in education than the current one. When the paper was presented to the governors, it was rejected thirty to three on the grounds that it still gave the federal government too big a role. It was tabled, and the governors are now reassessing their policy position.

We must go through a political process of sorting out responsibilities and priorities. I do believe that we should sort out those things which the federal government simply cannot do. The economic realities of the federal budget, regardless of who is president, are such that the federal role in financing education just will not last for many more years. I wish it were different, but that's how I read it.

The federal budget is increasingly taken up with entitlement programs, known as "uncontrollables". There is only about 24 percent of the budget which is available for so-called controllable or discretionary spending. But out of this comes the federal civilian payroll, the military payroll, much of the Department of Defense budget, and hundreds of human resource programs, among them education. The states now provide roughly 50 percent of the cost of K–12 education, and the trend has been toward increasing this proportion. I see a continued strong state role in education. It is important to understand, however, that although they rely on their state departments of education for leadership, more and more legislators, and governors too, are adding people who are knowledgeable about education to their staffs. They are taking a great interest in

7

education, and often come to believe that their ideas about it are just as good as those of the educators. In the short run, at least, the states will not be able to replace all of the dollars that are cut from the federal budget.

I believe that in the future, policy development at all levels will consider the common cause of education and its quality from the perspective of business and of national defense. The demographics mentioned earlier will have a large impact on both business and the military. The military will require about one-third of our high school graduates. Business will require its fair share, and the colleges and universities will be competing for those students. You can imagine who is going to win out. If we need people in the military, we are going have to pay them or draft them. Business wants the cream of the crop, and will pay whatever it takes to get them, including offering subsidized educational opportunities.

Finally, a few thoughts about schools and parents, or schools and citizens. National PTA people must be thinking about perhaps shifting the emphasis to a citizen and school approach instead of just a parent and teacher approach.

I have a philosophy—although I must admit that when I worked in Washington and at other times, I have not consistently behaved as if this *were* my philosophy—that parents have responsibility for the education of their children, and that the schools are a service organization that we have put together to help parents in that process. That is my ideal, and I believe that we should approach our problems from this base rather than feeling that the schools are somehow *intrinsically* important and that we must protect their role in society. Schools can't do it all. And we should stop acting, too, as if the schools were a closed system with some sort of monopoly on providing learning for our children. Another thing we should talk about is why the relationship between schools and parents are strained. A friend who is head of a national school volunteers organization admitted to me recently feeling intimidated in the schools. Why are the schools an intimidating environment? According to the best estimates I could get, only about 5 percent to 10 percent of the parents are involved in the schools. We have to reach beyond parents to make partners of all those who are interested in the schools, in education, from the growing human resource pool of singles, married couples without children, and retired people.

We need to improve the quality of teachers, and to not limit teaching to people with education majors. We need to implement what we know about effective schools, about which, fortunately, there is a growing consensus, recognizing such factors as: time on task-producing results; setting high expectations and having all the teachers subscribe to them; strong leadership, particularly at the building level; warm but businesslike environment; good evaluation and feedback to teachers; and rewards and encouragement to the good teachers we have.

As a society, we have no choice but to persist in trying to achieve quality, but we may need to make some new choices about how to achieve it. You and I can do a lot more than we are doing to make a difference and to help to direct change.

A School Administrator's Perspective
Verne A. Duncan

(Dr. Verne A. Duncan was elected to the post of State Superintendent of Public Instruction for the State of Oregon in November, 1974 and re-elected in 1978. As Executive Officer for the State Board of Education, which sets policies and goals for the state's public schools and community colleges, Dr. Duncan administers state-level programs that directly effect more than 700,000 students. Prior to assuming this position, Dr. Duncan taught in the classroom at all levels. He was also a principal at the elementary and junior high levels, a superintendent of schools in Idaho and a county superintendent in Oregon, as well as an assistant professor of educational administration at the University of Oregon. He served in the United States Army in 1956–58, and, in the Idaho House of Representatives during his stay there.

Dr. Duncan earned his M.Ed. in public school administration at the University of Idaho, his Ph.D. in public school administration at the University of Oregon in 1968, and an M.B.A. in business administration at the University of Portland in 1976.)

As we address the topic "Reading and Successful Living: The Family-School Partnership," a number of questions must be asked:

1. Is reading still important?
2. Why should there be cooperation between the family and the school?
3. What are the obstacles to establishing an effective family-school relationship?
4. How can the family and school work effectively together to improve children's reading skills?

This paper attempts to address these questions from the perspective of a school superintendent. If the call to action seems to place most of the responsibility for initiation on the shoulders of professional educators, it is because I believe that educators have been less than diligent in seeking family involvement in the educational process, and have in fact discouraged

Acknowledgment: The efforts of Ninette Florence, Reading Specialist, Oregon Department of Education, were instrumental in the development of this paper.

such involvement in the past. Parents are not without a major responsibility in this effort, but as the staff, hired by the public to manage the education system, it is part of the educator's duty to initiate the formation of a family-school partnership to improve the effectiveness of the education enterprise. That is what we are hired to do.

1. Is reading still important?

As the electronic media play an increasingly major part in the dissemination of information, there are those who maintain that the need to read is diminishing proportionately. A serious look at why we read reveals that this argument cannot be sustained. Reading is an integral part of our existence in each of the six life roles we all experience; those of the individual, lifelong learner, producer, citizen, consumer, and family member.

As individuals, we clarify our own personal values through reading the thoughts of others. We solve our personal problems by reading of the experiences of others in similar situations. This reading is necessary to obtain the depth necessary to allow us to make decisions about who and what we are and want to be, and what we want to believe and why. Appropriate depth is not available through the electronic media.

As lifelong learners, reading is imperative for us because the knowledge gained through the evolution of our entire civilization has been committed to paper and the printed word. If we are to continue to learn throughout our lives, new information, whether it is received auditorily or visually, must be evaluated in the context of history and experience, as documented in print.

As producers, our ability to continue to grow in our jobs is dependent upon keeping abreast of the changes in the state of the art of our occupations, be they blue collar or white collar. The impact of technological advances has affected every profession, and the new strategies, methodologies and techniques are most often disseminated through trade journals and manuals where we can read of them and evaluate their potential for improving our own productivity.

As citizens, reading is our safeguard against being unduly influenced by political advertising. Without the ability to read and evaluate information about candidates and issues, our only

11

source of information becomes the electronic media. They do not provide the depth nor the objectivity we need upon which to base decisions.

As consumers, it is essential that we be able to compare the products we purchase. Again, only through reading can we assure ourselves that we have the objective information necessary to assure our safety and well-being. We certainly cannot rely upon paid commercials as our sole source of product information.

As family members we must understand the occurrences around us that affect our families, and be able to discuss the outside influences which force us into family-related decisions involving economics, employment, religion, education, housing, family planning, etc.

Betsy Mynhier, Reading Consultant with the Kentucky Department of Education, in a paper published by the National Institute of Education put it well:

> "In spite of the competition from the mass media of today, reading continues to increase in importance in the American way of life. As our society continues to grow in technological discovery, more and more types of reading are required. The role of the reading teacher is magnified as he guides boys and girls in applying techniques of critical evaluation of reading to what is seen and heard on radio and television and what is read from the vast amount of printed books, magazines, and newspapers.
>
> "The printed page is many things to many people. Reading a book can be a visit to the moon, a means of discovery and awakening, or a euphoria for unleashed emotions and interests. Reading is essential to the existence of our complex system of social arrangement. It is the means by which the past can be relived, arguments and beliefs can be expressed, forms of government can be understood, and generations can be linked to the history of mankind. Truly, reading is the bond that brings people and places together."[1]

[1]Mynhier, Betsy, Reading Consultant, Kentucky Department of Education, James B. Graham, Superintendent, *Parents Are Reading Teachers Too!*, U.S. Department of Health, Education and Welfare, National Institute of Education, Washington, DC, May 1981.

As we move into a world of computerization, with technology that automatically corrects our misspelling, grammatical errors, and poor punctuation, there is the danger of becoming over-armed with and overly dependent upon computers. As personal computers become commonplace in American homes we must emphasize the sheer joy of reading as well as its practical applications. The new technology may be able to handle the greatly increased amount of information available, but the final determination about what to do with it requires the ability to think critically, to reason and to make value judgments and still rests with us. Skill in developing and exercising these abilities can be gained through reading. Reading as it contributes to life roles in successful living is one important consideration, but the ultimate goal is for each individual to recognize the breadth and added dimension reading can give to the quality of life. In fact, if we as educators do our job right we would not only emphasize the concept of "read to live" but develop the love of reading to the extent that students would want to "live to read."

2. Why cooperation between family and school?

A recent report by the Governor's Task Force on Effective Schooling in Alaska makes an important distinction between education and schooling in defining the role of the schools:

> "The Task Force adopted the position that education is
> a responsibility of society as a whole—parents and
> other family members, community members, churches,
> media, agencies, and the school—whereas schooling is
> the responsibility of the school. Schooling was defined
> as the process of being taught in a school, or the process
> of providing instruction in a structured setting.
> Responsibilities of schools were regarded according to
> three differing categories, which were:
> 1. Primary—the providing of schooling—instruction—in
>   basic skills, content and other skill areas comprising
>   the curriculum, and providing leadership in effecting
>   positive relationships with parents, the community,
>   and groups within the community.
> 2. Shared–providing instruction in skill or content areas
>   in conjunction with groups, agencies, or private indus-
>   try, as well as modeling and encouraging the develop-

ment of behaviors and attitudes for which there exists general community support.

3. Supportive–maintaining a supportive relationship with those individuals and groups apart from the school which have primary responsibilities for education."[2]

Often overlooked is the fact that the family members are in fact the child's primary teachers. From the moment a child is born he or she is learning from family members. We teach a child about communications when we respond with food or attention to a cry. It is the family which teaches values, language, walking, and other basic skills during those first five most critical learning years, both by active instruction and by modeling. It is the parents who influence a child the most. Therefore, it is parents who are the most effective teachers.

Our philosophy is in error when we discuss how to involve parents in the work of the school. More important is establishing the role of the parent as teacher, and then determining how the school can help in the work of the parent. Rather than parents serving as teacher aides, perhaps we should view teachers as parent aides. It is carrying things too far, however, to assume that parents are the *only* teachers. The increasing number of children being educated at home is an overreaction to the realization that the school alone cannot effectively teach children. We must find the middle ground based on the realization that education is a shared responsibility. Most will concede to schools a technical expertise beyond what is available in the home. Yet to be effective, this expertise must be imparted to a receptive mind. This receptivity is influenced to a great extent by the environment in the home, both positively and negatively.

The *NEWS*, by Basic Skills National Technical Assistance Consortium, summarizes studies on the importance of community and school level characteristics for student achievement. According to their data, one factor had a decisive effect: "The extent of involvement and interest by parents in school policies and in their childrens' academic performance." They also quote Benjamin Bloom's generalization that "Where the home and school are mutually enforcing environments, the child's educa-

---

[2]The Governor's Task Force on Effective Schooling, *Effective Schooling Practices, A Report to the Governor,* Juneau, Alaska, August 1981.

tional and social development are likely to take place at higher and higher levels."[3]

Research shows that the home environment has a strong positive relationship to reading achievement. The conclusion is that the home environment is a prominent factor in explaining the attitudes children take toward reading, and in determining their reading success in school. The Coleman Report further substantiates this.

In Affective Parent Education in Philadelphia, Jessie M. Gibson concludes: "In short, it is very apparent that the family, and the parents in particular, are powerful influences on the child's learning even before the child reaches school. The family is a place where children learn first, and the extent to which they learn later in life is determined greatly by what goes on in the home."[4]

With the importance of the parent and family firmly established in the educational process, attention must be turned to harnessing the immense influence of the home to a positive educational end—teaching parents to teach.

In Parents, Children, and Reading, Pickarts and DeFranco state: "The parent often has little awareness that he is teaching his child in many ways through the constant parent-child interaction. Although he may view himself as a teacher of morals, proper behavior, honesty and courtesy, it is unlikely that he will know he is teaching the important things that provide the base for learning to read—teaching through the provision of experiences and his own reactions to the child. Furthermore, even when he sees himself as an important teacher of his child, he may not have the understanding and skill to apply to the task."[5]

Parents teach but are rarely taught to teach. Their approaches are derived from one or more sources. Most often, perhaps, they pattern their teaching upon the way in which their patents taught them. If they were punished for not learning, they punish. What they carry over from what they have experienced may or may not be in line with what we know today about

[3]"Focus: Some Issues in Parent Involvement," NEWS, Vol. 1, No. 4 (1981), The Basic Skills National Technical Assistance Consortium, CEMREL, Inc., St. Louis, Missouri.

[4]Gibson, Jessie M., Affective Parent Education in Philadelphia, School District of Philadelphia, Philadelphia, Pennsylvania, 1978.

[5]Pickarts, Evelyn M., and Ellen B. DeFranco, Parents, Children, and Reading, A Handbook for Teachers, New York: American Book Company, 1972.

learning. What they do may be even less compatible with the realities of today, for their memories of what and how they learned may not be accurate. Traditional beliefs become a folklore of what should be done, and are rarely tested against the scientific knowledge of the present. Finally, there is always the impact of the barrage of advice, often contradictory and not always sound, that pours forth upon them from the mass media.

We can be certain that the parent will teach his child, either knowingly or unknowingly. The only question is: "Should he do it intuitively and without insight or with knowledge and understanding?" The obvious conclusion is that perhaps our education system would do better educating children if we spent more time educating parents.

3. What are the obstacles to establishing an effective family–school relationship?

The primary obstacle is our penchant for convenience. It is more convenient for educators to develop and implement programs unilaterally than otherwise, and more convenient for parents to allow the school to do so. What we lack is the essential commitment by educators and parents to relinquish convenience for the sake of effectiveness. We educators have become masters of using advisory committees, task forces, or public surveys when it serves our own purposes. Historically, such efforts have had more public relations value than educational value, and topics for discussion have been deftly steered away from substantive issues.

On the other hand, parents have historically settled for token involvement, because substantive involvement entails a great deal of time and energy, not to mention an increased level of stress and frustration, of which most of us have adequate amounts in our own personal lives. The excuses used by both parents and educators to justify this token involvement are imbedded in our very life-styles. We don't have enough time, as parents, to become so involved in our child's "school problems"; the schools don't have enough money to conduct a parent involvement program; and, many more weak excuses which we, as parents and educators, have heard over and over.

We no longer hold the underlying belief that the most important thing we can do is educate children. We have rationalized it away with economic and social justifications. To some parents it is more important to work overtime so the child can buy designer jeans than it is to spend those extra hours reading with the child. To some educators it is more important to have the latest body-building equipment in the locker rooms than to have a parent involvement program which may improve educational effectiveness. By mutual consent we've settled for less than the best education for our children, and that is a crime against them and our future society.

4. How can the family and school work effectively together to improve children's reading?

First, educators and parents must believe that:

- Reading skills can be improved through a cooperative effort.
- The improvement of reading skills is important enough to warrant the extra effort involved.
- Both parents and educators are sincerely interested in cooperating to improve children's reading skills.

Naturally, the question arises, "Who should take the initiative?" I believe the school must, and the following are some steps which should be taken to facilitate establishment of a parent-school relationship:

1. The school superintendent should help the board establish formal policies for the inclusion of parents as regular and necessary participants in the instructional process.

2. These policies should be developed in a cooperative effort between the school and parents. The policies, once adopted, must be reflected in the district and program goals, curriculum guides, and actual classroom instruction. Neither districts nor parents should feel restricted as to the scope of involvement because of historic attitudes or past practices based on federal program regulations.

3. A wide range of participation modes should be established so that all parents can find a way to participate that is compatible with their schedules and interests.

4. District administrators must clearly communicate the policy to principals and teachers. In fact, it is imperative that building level staff be involved in its development. The commitment must be felt throughout the system.

5. Staff and budget must be allocated to this purpose to assure the policies become more than just words on paper. This program must become a regular part of the planning and budgeting process. This does not mean that all funds must necessarily be tax funds. Private contributions for these purposes may be available from local businesses, industries, and community based groups. For example, in one Oregon city a local corporation paid for the development and distribution of a handbook for parents of all three-year-old children in the district.

6. The staff should keep in mind that parents are more interested in participation if they can see it linked directly to their own children's achievement in reading. This is an important planning consideration.

7. Mutual accessibility—school to the parents, and parents to the school staff—must be provided.

8. Communications between home and school, through all available means, should be established. A wide variety of communication tools are available, including: PTAs, Parents in Classroom programs, teacher visits to home, newspaper articles to help parents, television and radio spots, letters to parents, public library programs, open houses, parent-teacher coffees, classes at businesses, stores, and union meetings.

9. Parents must feel welcome in the school building. Too many parents feel as if they are intruding when they enter a school. Both parents and educators must remember that the school belongs to the public. The public just hires educators to occupy it.

10. "In-home involvement" must be encouraged. This is where there is the most time and opportunity for parents to build oral language, and a background of experiences. Dorothy Rich, testifying in 1979, cited the fact that parents have true concern for their children's achievement and they possess abilities to help. She also stated that schools should start their programs with what the family has, instead of worrying so much about what it doesn't have or hasn't done. "Schools, no matter how understaffed, have the capabilities of reaching out and effecting parent involvement, using easy, inexpen-

sive materials, and without waiting for what probably won't come—organizational change or massive government funding."[6]

11. Schools should provide materials so parents can help with the instruction. These materials can take a variety of forms:

    a. Teachers can send reading books home after students complete them at school. Books from the school library can also be sent home. There are the paperback giveaway programs such as those that have been sponsored by the Reading Is Fundamental program. These programs can also be sponsored by public libraries, PTAs, or other organizations.

    b. Children's books can be taken to major factories, offices, and places of business. Paperbacks can be put in laundromats, post offices, unemployment offices, doctor offices, and other likely locations. We must be as creative as possible, placing books where parents spend their time and have time to look at them.

    c. Other inexpensive materials for parents to use are those items that are already in the home, such as newspapers, recipe books, labels, magazines, manuals, and directions for putting together games.

    d. Schools can provide parents with the companion tutoring material to the school's reading series and keep them posted as to what lessons to do at home.

12. Schools must provide help to parents on how to instruct children:

    a. Specific tutor training workshops can be provided for parents working in the school setting prior to their working with children. The Right to Read tutor training program recommends that parents, or any volunteer, be provided with enough background in reading instruction to understand the objectives of lessons for which they are providing practice. Also, parents should be given some specific instruction on how to read to children and on the basic instruc-

---

[6]Rich, Dorothy, *The Home and School Institute, Testimony on the Basic Skills Improvement Program Authorized Under Title II of the Education Amendments of 1978*, presented to the Regional Commissioner for Educational Programs, Department of HEW, Region III, Philadelphia, Pennsylvania, May 1979.

19

tional philosophy of the reading series being used in the school. The training should also deal with responses to children's remarks or complaints, how to motivate children, and how to use the library. A training program such as this makes the tutor feel much more confident when working with children, both at school and on their own at home.

For parents working with their children at home:

- All materials sent home should have an accompanying note explaining what and how help is to be given. This helps parents feel more confident that what they are doing is correct.
- Schools can provide outlines of what is being taught, and when, so parents can supplement.
- Educational programs for parents can be provided by the schools during the day or evening, at school, in libraries, in business offices and plants, stores, or community centers. The most effective programs are series in which parents have the opportunity to reflect on their own concerns and have their questions answered.
- Schools can distribute parent booklets. This can be done as a massive campaign, as a part of parent-teacher conferences, or to the parents of all students as they enter school at various levels.
- Schools can have classes for older children to teach them to read to, or help, younger children. This is good both for family members and for baby-sitters. This can also be incorporated in a regular part of the school program.
- Schools can provide instruction as a part of another activity—sports events, school plays, etc.
- Television series can be developed on how to help your children read. Schools can also send home a list of pertinent television programs, including suggestions on how to view and discuss them with children.
- Instructional tapes can be sent home.

Instruction for parents should include, among other things, help with:

a. building oral language
b. reading orally to children
c. listening to a child read
d. helping with homework
e. knowing the fundamentals of reading
f. identifying games to play at home
g. the selection of good books
h. identifying components of a home environment that fosters reading
13. Schools can provide motivation for parents to want to be involved:
   a. They must provide evidence that what parents do really helps. This involves setting up an evaluation system that is more than just numbers. The bottom line is, do the children read better with the help of the parents? Frequent reports to the parents will let them know.
   b. Various statewide or district-wide campaigns might help. The Oregon Governor and I sponsored a summer reading program, offering certificates signed by us for children who read ten or more books during the summer. Thousands of students have maintained their reading skills over the summer months as a result of this incentive, and teachers have noticed the difference in September.
   c. Various awards or forms of recognition can be presented. *Parents in Reading,* published by Northwest Regional Educational Laboratory,[7] provides ideas for efforts to get parents to read to their children every day.

If communication can take place, perception changes to one of shared responsibility: parents are provided with materials and ideas for using them, and a real partnership can and should follow.

The most important factor in the change in attitudes on the part of parents and educators is the realization that schooling is only a part of education. Reading is a prime example of an area where shared responsibility can increase educational effectiveness.

---

[7]Northwest Regional Educational Laboratory, *Parents In Reading,* Administrators Guide, Portland, Oregon, 1979.

What has been described here is a program with parents as active partners with the schools. Optimism and theory are great. When tempered by reality, however, we must admit that not all parents will become involved in such an active partnership. The growing number of single parent and dual breadwinner families dictates limitations on the time parents will spend in an active educational effort. At the very least we should expect all parents to be passive partners with the schools. Even the parent with very little time to spend with a child can instill an attitude of importance about what the school is doing, and a sense of excitement about the joy of reading.

As we address the family-school partnership, our obvious preference is for an active partnership, but we will have taken a giant step toward educational effectiveness if we can enlist the currently nonactive parents into at least a passive partnership.

For too long we have settled for less than excellence in the education of our children. Excellence can be achieved—in reading, and other areas, but it takes a determination on the part of all of society to believe it can happen, and to take the actions necessary to make excellence occur. It takes the various components of society working together to achieve excellence—or, as we in Oregon put it—an "Alliance for Excellence." Society must rediscover the importance of education and dedicate itself to a renewed commitment to our young people—a commitment to participate as a full partner in the education process—and a commitment to participation in the Alliance for Excellence.

RESPONSES AND DISCUSSION

In his remarks introducing discussion of his paper, Verne Duncan highlighted some of its major points. He emphasized that the Alliance for Excellence mentioned at the end of his paper is not just an alliance of schools and parents but of the entire community bent on quality education, because "Education is too important to be left to the educators." He urged listeners to reject *firmly* whenever it comes up, in speeches or conversation, the notion that reading will not continue to be important in many aspects of peoples' lives.

As to encouraging parents, families, and schools to work

together to improve children's reading, Dr. Duncan stressed that it is essential that people understand that improvement can take place, and that their involvement can help it to take place. Also, a wide range of participation modes must be established so that parents can find a way to participate that is compatible with their schedules, their interests, and their abilities. Staff must bear in mind that parents are more interested in participation if they can see that it is linked directly with their own children's achievement in reading. He reaffirmed the great importance of constant communication so that parents and families feel that they know what is going on and feel comfortable in dealing with the school. Also, plan to use what the family has, and don't worry about what it doesn't have.

KARL PLATH, *Superintendent of Township High School, District #113, Highland Park, Illinois,* was the first respondent to Dr. Duncan. He affirmed that in the light of his experience, initiative in family-school collaboration matters has to come from the administration of the school district. What is the family in 1981? Dr. Plath pointed out that in 1980 one of every five children lived with only one parent. By 1990, one in four will live with one parent. Compared with 1960, when only one in eleven children lived with one parent, the picture is shifting fast. Even Webster's definition of a family, "a body of persons who live in one household," may not serve as well in the future when family members, though linked in other ways, may not all live together under one roof. At present, the majority of boys and girls still do live with parents and siblings, but the percentage is decreasing rapidly due to divorce, separation, remarriage, and a shift from the nuclear to the extended family.

Care has been taken in Dr. Plath's district to employ staff at all levels who can identify with different groups. The staffs of the schools work with parents who cannot read themselves so that they can become role models and help children actively. Dr. Plath expressed hope that a real action plan can emerge from the symposium and that it can receive wide circulation. There are one thousand school districts in Illinois alone, each with their own PTAs, Dad's Clubs, and business communities, representing a vast potential for the kind of alliance Verne Duncan talked about. But this potential will mean nothing unless it is stirred to action. Materials need to go to statewide organizations and to consortia of educational leadership at the state level so that agencies and organizations can play a supporting role in developing a family-school partnership for reading development in local communities. City systems are quite different from suburban and rural school systems and must be approached differently.

The question of money to support even basic operation of the schools, as well as innovative programs of any kind, must be solved in various ways—in whatever ways are appropriate and possible in given situations. He cited Dr. Ruth Love, a former reading teacher and Director of the National Right to Read Program who is now superintendent of schools in Chicago, and her successful efforts to tap foundations and the business community for funds. Beverly Hills, California, while hardly a typical suburban community, has augmented local funds with a foundation grant of $500,000. We can learn from these efforts.

Dr. Plath affirmed strongly that education—and reading, often symbolic of education as one of its chief tools—be kept on the national agenda of issues and priorities affecting all the people, however they are to be funded.

MARY ANN LEVERIDGE, *National President of PTA*

Mrs. Leveridge pointed out that many members of PTA are professionals in education as well as parents. She herself has reared five children and is an elected member of the Texas State Board of Education.

At its inception, the PTA was not associated with schools; it was the National Congress of Mothers. Now most of the 27,000 local units are associated with public school campuses, a unique relationship sponsored in effect by the superintendents of schools. There are some parochial, private, and even preschool PTAs affiliated with the national organization, but most relate to the public schools. People who work in PTAs are generally very supportive of the school system. Individuals may be outspokenly critical and occasionally hostile about specific situations, but as a group they have a great deal of respect for what appears to have been, until now, the school system's primary goal: to bring all of the children of all of the people within its reach.

NPTA is a broadbased volunteer organization, with no vested interest in any particular aspect of education, but it is a prime vehicle for doing what this conference is about. "Our

24

biggest fault is that we have not brought into our organization the millions of parents out there who do not belong and have little association with their schools. If we are to be successful, we must make extra efforts to being these people in and train our parents to have more input into education. Advisory councils of parents or citizens, however mandated, are generally rubber stamps for education officials."

Now we also need to address achievement. We need a formalized process to measure reading achievement. "I have not found any group of parents in all of my travels around this country who do not feel that the very base, the very foundation of all learning, is reading. It is interesting to me in listening to PTA groups to find that parents recognize that mastery of essential reading skills in the early grades is critical and important, but it is not enough. They also have a very real concern for the area now exposed by the national assessment of educational progress, which shows that children are not mastering the skills to synthesize, to analyze, and to achieve the higher level thinking skills. I am even hearing a little, I believe, that perhaps the emphasis on back-to-basics has gotten in the way of emphasis on these other things. We need to look at teacher education, at in-service development, and make it essential for teachers at the secondary level as well as at the primary level to know how to teach reading, and how to motivate students to develop the higher level reading/thinking skills that are so necessary to survival in our society."

A great deal of the talk that occurs at every meeting has to do with technology. "We must learn to think of technology in its proper place: technologies become additional tools, but they are not going to replace teachers. And they make it more important than ever that we have early mastery of some of the skills of reading and English language arts for critical thinking, critical viewing and critical listening which adults must have to succeed in a world where they are constantly bombarded with information."

There has been much rhetoric in the past about communication between the family and the schools. There are schools that are doing this very effectively. "From what I have seen, the school administrators who truly believe that the public schools belong to the people are doing the best job of it. They have the leadership skills to involve the community—not just the parents of children in the schools, but organizations, labor unions, businesses. They are not afraid of parents who come to the school because they have the skills to deal with them. They are also providing the same kinds of skills for their teachers so that they can cope with the involvement of the community in the school. If we would analyze the success rate of bond issues in those areas where this takes place, we would find that they have been successful where support is concerned. There is an important lesson here for all of us."

But if there is going to be meaningful parent involvement in a society where we have two working parents and one-parent families where the one parent has to work, we have to plan differently from the way we have in the past. People are not going to come to school unless they are asked to address something substantive that is really going to make a difference in their lives and the lives of their children. Perhaps we need to look at some new ways to gain access to some of these people— school systems as well as PTAs. "In Texas, we have a business which came to the state PTA and asked if we would come into their plants and organize plant PTAs. They give their parents who have children in school time off to attend meetings. The school system involved comes to those meetings and offers orientation and parent training, as they do in other PTA meetings. This might lead to a change in organization to accommodate broad community involvement of non-parents as well as parents."

Lack of trust has always been an obstacle. "We need to make some extraordinary efforts to get parents to trust teachers—and teachers must be trustworthy for this to happen. If a parent goes to a school with a problem about a child, and wants to know what to do at home to help, and the teacher says—and believe me, it often happens, and it is still happening—'we're doing fine; we don't really need your help,' that ends the discussion, and that's bad. We can't tolerate it anymore. Parents are becoming increasingly activist about demanding what they want in the schools, and when this kind of thing happens there is one more person out there who is not a friend of the school and will not be supportive of it. It will require some inservice training of teachers to teach them the skills for dealing with hostile parents when they do come in, and also to provide them with some specific ways to get parents into the school in non-hostile situations, and not just when they have a problem. It can be done properly. I see schools all the time where it is done well, largely due to the leadership of the local campus principal. One way to bring more parents into schools is to get the kids to want them to come and let them do the recruiting themselves. I am told this does not work at the secondary level, but it does—its just that nobody has tried it much."

In one school district where they identified children who scored low, they developed a formal plan for working with the parents of these children to help the parents to help the children improve. After home visits to parents of sixth, seventh, and eighth-graders, seven sessions of two hours each were held for parent training. Parents were trained in positive parenting techniques, informal reading inventories, sight word strategies, asking questions, and recording their interaction with the child or children. Each parent agreed to work with the student for ten minutes every day, to listen to him read, to learn new words, to check fluency and to ask questions for comprehension. One of the things they encountered was that some parents could not read or write. This was a real problem. They gave those parents tape recorders to use. Parents met with the teacher once, and at the end of nine months, the achievement status in reading, as well as in writing and in math—which the sessions did not even address—rose by two grade levels. One of the peripheral benefits of this program was that the parents who participated in it for the duration learned many skills for participating in society which they previously lacked. They also developed a greatly enhanced self-image and began to get involved in activities in which they had never been involved before.

"One of the most important questions is how do we define educating children? Who is going to define that? In Texas we have been working for the past two years trying to understand what it is that the people of the state—not just the parents, but the business and industry and political groups—think that the schools should be doing. It might surprise some people, especially those who say that the school cannot be all things to all people, to know that that doesn't appear to reflect what people want. People seem to think that the school *must* be everything to children, because there are so many children in our society for whom the schools provide the only access to the mainstream society and its values—whether the schools like it or not. The schools must confront this or they will not be able to produce in the area of academic achievement. *We need to devise a specific, formalized process to widen the circle of citizens—not just parents—who are involved in schools and in deciding what kind of job the community wants the schools to do.*"

Comments from floor discussion. "It is important to start with the very young child, and to read to the child from at least the age of two; that's when language begins to be important and that's when it is easiest to get parents involved." (Marian Brown)

"Schools need to believe more firmly that most parents want to help, but often don't know how. The schools should be doing something to make them feel capable of helping and supporting children's reading." (Barbara Rollock)

"Foreign language parents must be assured that oral language is important as a basis for reading in any laguage. Also, not only parents can read to or listen to younger children. Older brothers and sisters can also. Family-wide participation is needed. An older sibling, for example, might speak both English and Spanish, while the parents may only speak Spanish. The fifth grader, in a family where both parents work, may be the one who is most at home with a younger child." (Nancy Larrick)

A Reading Teacher's Perspective
Leo Fay

(Dr. Leo C. Fay has been associated with the School of Education at Indiana University for more than twenty-five years, and is chairman of the Reading Education Department and professor of education. He has served as president of the International Reading Association, as co-director of the ERIC Clearinghouse on Reading (ERIC/CRIER), and on numerous boards, commissions, and task forces concerned with reading and with the education of teachers. He is the author of several well-known reading series for young people and professional books for educators. He was co-director of the Indiana study on reading, Then and Now, which compared reading achievement of the 1940s with that of the 1970s in Indiana schools.

Dr. Fay earned both his master's degree and his doctorate in education at the University of Minnesota, and taught in his home state and in New York state prior to his appointment at Indiana. He has lectured and taught at colleges and universities around the world, including assignments as visiting professor in Thailand and Pakistan. He is in great demand as a consultant, and he is the recipient of the Herman Frederick Lieber Award for Distinguished Teaching at Indiana University.)

In the daily course of events it is all too easy to get caught up in the routines of keeping school, and, in the process, lose sight of the larger issues that underlie effective schooling. Virginia Mathews has a knack for periodically seeing to it that the larger questions are considered. A decade ago she was instrumental in organizing two conferences dealing with major issues of reading in our society. One conference, held at Indiana University in connection with its sesquicentennial celebration ceremony (1970) was concerned with "Reading and the National Interest." The second, held in Chicago, jointly sponsored by the International Reading Association and the American Book Publishers Council was called "Reading and Revolution, The Role of Reading in Today's Society." Once again she has us casting a critical eye on what is and reflecting as to what might be done to further enhance reading.

29

While the primary concern of this paper is to discuss reading instruction, it is important to have some understanding of the development of literacy in our nation and of the present status of reading achievement in our schools.

The concern for increasing literacy following World War I, the enforcement of attendance laws, and the steady increase in the holding power of the schools were primary factors in the literacy gains. For example, only 6 percent of seventeen-year-olds completed high school in 1900; this increased to 17 percent in 1920, 51 percent in 1940, 65 percent in 1960, and 75 percent in 1965. No further increase has been made since for seventeen-year-olds. However, the various military and adult education programs now result in 86 percent of twenty-five-year-olds holding a high school diploma or its equivalent. At the same time the proportion of young people attending degree-granting colleges has increased to the point that it is greater today than the proportion completing high school a generation ago. Obviously, the educational base of the country has grown substantially over time.

Some would claim that this has been accomplished by lowering standards and even by permitting illiterates to graduate from high school. This simply is not so. In his discussion of functional literacy among seventeen-year-olds, Donald Fisher, in *Functional Literacy and the Schools*, comments "(the) analysis suggests that schools are more effective today than they have been over the last thirty to forty years. . . . Specifically, we found that one might reasonably conclude that the high schools were graduating very, very few functional illiterates. It could well be the case that the functional illiteracy rate among high school graduates is significantly less than one percent."[1] (Table A–15, p. 47—reports 0.7 percent)

It is difficult to convince people that schools are, in the main, effective. Most attention from the media is negative, and the truth is that the public has never been totally pleased with its schools. The young, from the days of Socrates to the present, have never seemed to measure up to what their elders would like them to do or to be. People see the shortcomings of the present, remember the past with a halo, and conclude that conditions are worsening on the basis of impressions rather than real evidence.

---

[1]Fisher, Donald L. *Functional Literacy and the Schools*, Washington, D.C.: National Institute of Education, HEW, January, 1978.

The accomplishments that distinguish America today are built upon an ever improving educational base.

The importance of the basic ability to read in our society can hardly be overstated although its relative importance may vary markedly from one person to another. Recent research performed at Indiana University[2] and at Purdue University[3] indicates that nearly every job (98 percent of those surveyed) has some literacy requirement, that the average amount of time spent reading on a job exceeds two hours daily, and that the average difficulty of work and functional literacy materials ranges from tenth to twelfth-grade level. A substantial number of individuals, though technically literate, are kept from advancement in employment because of inadequacies in functional literacy. How serious a problem this is is debatable. It can be argued, as Newman has, that the American work force is becoming increasingly over-educated in relation to the skill demands of most occupations.[4] While skill demands may be at the tenth to twelfth-grade levels, the tasks are typically highly repetitive and are easily mastered by most individuals on the job. Also of relevance is the fact that in 1980 the nation reached the point where half of its factory workers had a high school diploma.

What Should Schools Accomplish. As we face the future of American schooling, we sorely need to address the issue of realistic expectations for schools and learners. Obviously, people differ; hence it is reasonable to expect differences in achievement. In our society, an expectation of basic functional literacy is a reasonable goal for essentially all students. An analysis of the National Assessment data released in May 1981 suggests that this goal has been met for those in school.

Beyond that, expectations more properly should be individualized. Gertrude Hildreth once commented that about half of the children have some difficulty in learning to read. She then described three groups of children: the bookish and highly verbal who take to reading like ducks to water; the concrete-

[2]Mikulecky, Larry J. Job Literacy: The Relationship Between School Preparation and Workplace Actuality—Final Report, February, 1981. National Institute of Education, NIE-G-79-0168, Washington, D.C.

[3]Moe, Alden J., R. Timothy Rush and Rebecca L. Storlie. *The Literacy Requirements of an Electrician on the Job and in a Vocational Training Program,* Department of Education, Purdue University, January, 1980 (A series of ten different occupations).

[4]Newman, Dorothy K. and Associates, "Learning Without Earning," *Change,* March, 1978 pp. 38–43 and 60.

minded, often labeled as slow learners, who experience great difficulty with reading, and struggle to achieve basic literacy; and the practical-minded—children who can learn, but who need to be motivated and carefully directed. Children in this last group recognize reading as a useful tool, and master its use, but they would rather, under most conditions, do other things than read. The issue of differential expectation for children in these three groups is critical, but largely ignored.

Perhaps our difficulties, particularly with our secondary schools, reflect a lack of realistically dealing with the question of expectation. It often appears that many critics will never be satisfied with less than a Ph.D. for everyone. Ignoring this issue may be a major reason for the absence of progress in reducing the school dropout rate over the last sixteen years. Defining expectation is a major challenge for the immediate future, with important implications for the curriculum, the nature of instruction, and the general keeping of school. This is no simple issue: both quality and diversity are involved.

Having made the point that a basically sound educational program is in place and that it is important, if not critical, to give serious consideration to what reasonable expectations for reading achievement might be, it is useful to review the results of the National Assessment of Educational Progress in reading.[5] This test assesses reading in three broad categories: literal comprehension, inferential comprehension, and use of reference skills. Thus the National Assessment defines reading as comprehension.

The NAEP tests were administered in the school years 1970–71, 1974–75, and 1979–80 to a broad sample of nine, thirteen, and seventeen-year-olds representing all geographic sections of the country. The sample included systematically selected males, females, students from majority and minority racial groups, students whose parents had achieved varying levels of education, and students from communities of various types and sizes.

The test questions included reading tasks representing both in-school and out-of-school reading activities. The tests were developed to reflect the important goals of reading as deter-

[5]Farr, Roger. *Reading Achievement in Our Nation's Schools.* A Testimony before the House Subcommittee on Elementary, Secondary and Vocational Education, Washington, D.C., April 29, 1981.

mined by a panel of educators and lay people. Thus for the first time reliable, systematically gathered information has been accumulated over time to determine reading achievement and possible trends in performance. Hopefully here we now have the basis for moving beyond impressions and misinterpretations based upon inadequate data. An analysis of the National Assessment data over a decade is quite revealing and has important implications for instruction. What do the data show?

First, the results reveal a pattern of increasing achievement for nine and thirteen-year-olds in all categories and for seventeen-year-olds in literal comprehension and reference skills, and a small decline in inferential comprehension. Over the age groups the gain in literal comprehension is large and the decline in inferential comprehension small.

Second, the largest increases are among those populations which have been the primary focus of supplementary education programs. These groups include the youngest students and those most educationally and socioeconomically deprived. Obviously, the Title programs have made a difference.

Third, the stability and relative lack of improvement in reading achievement among the thirteen and seventeen-year-olds suggests that extra effort is needed at these levels if improvements similar to those at the nine-year level can be expected.

Fourth, the decline of inferential reading skills among seventeen-year-olds exists primarily among the most able students. The group with the greatest decline lives in the Northeastern States, in advantaged urban communities and with parents who have the greatest amount of education. In spite of the decline, this group remains the highest achieving of all groups tested. Thus, the National Assessment results suggest that the basic reading skills of school age children are improving and that we may be at a national all-time high in basic literacy achievement. The decline of inferential skills among seventeen-year-olds may be the consequence of students learning to read but not expanding and developing their reading skills at the most advanced levels.

Implications for Instruction. *In a sentence, the National Assessment data suggest that the schools' problems with reading are not with the minimums but rather with higher levels of performance.* Yet for some reason, otherwise rational people have mandated school programs that essentially insure mediocrity. The advocates of back-to-basics instruction demand increased time for the so-called basic skills and the reduction, if not elimination, of curriculum areas and activities that would require higher level applications of reading skills. *The issue is not the presence or absence of instruction to build basic reading competency but rather to provide the opportunity to apply skills in increasingly demanding situations.* Skills become sharper as the process of reading or writing is applied than they do when taught in isolation.

Nevertheless, periodically the demand arises for a return to basic skills or minimum essentials. This happened in the mid-thirties, with many schools doing little more than working through pads of drill material on minimum essentials. Prior to that, in the teens, the schools went through a similar experience. In reaction to the movement then, Thorstein Veblen, writing in 1918, observed, "The underlying presumption appears to be that learning is a commodity to be produced on a piece rate plan, rated, measured, and counted and reduced to staple equivalents by impersonal, mechanical tests. In all its bearing the work is hereby reduced to a mechanistic, statistical consistency, with numerical standards and units, which conduces to perfunctory and mediocre work throughout, and acts to deter both students and teachers from a free pursuit of knowledge."[6]

This sounds all too familiar. Time and again teachers tell me, "Our greatest problem is that we are not permitted to teach. We are putting all of our energy into minutia imposed upon us—testing, diagnosing, playing with bits and pieces, and reporting it all to the central office. All we do is serve a monster system that thrives on trivia. We do not teach and children do not learn." In all of this—the competencies, the behavioral objectives, the assumption that nothing is learned unless it can be measured, the management systems—we are in danger of being overwhelmed by a big-brother-knows-best type of conformity that never really permits the full blossoming of what education can be for the development of people.

What we are dealing with is an issue that has plagued education ever since schooling became organized and formalized. Over time the language changes—open versus closed, logical versus psychological, skill versus process, child centered

---

[6]Veblen, Thorstein. "The Higher Learning in America: A Memorandum on the Conduct of Universities by Businessmen." New York, 1918.

versus curriculum centered, the ends versus the means. Carlyle's essay, *Pedagogy* (1830s) suggests the basic nature of the problem in these words:

> My teachers were hidebound pedants without knowledge of man's nature, or of boy's; or of ought save their lexicons and quarterly account books. Innumerable dead vocables they crammed into us, and called it fostering the growth of mind. How can an inanimate, mechanical gerund-grinder, the like of whom will, in a subsequent century, be manufactured at Nuremberg out of wood and leather foster the growth of anything; much more of mind which grows, not like a vegetable by having its roots littered with etymological compost, but like a spirit, by mysterious contact of spirit. . . . How shall he give kindling, in whose inward mind there is no live coal, but all is burnt out to a dead grammatical cinder.[7]

Carlyle may have provided at least a partial answer to the question of why this emphasis on skills happens. It is easier for the teacher because the learning situation is under tight control—with the learner passive rather than active. Perhaps part of the answer is political. People who can think can be dangerous. In any event, over the last decade we have become overly caught up in the ends of education. This is what can be easily measured and accounted for. These ends are seen as subject matter to be learned—the gerunds that so upset Carlyle. The textbook, the curriculum, the schedule, and the fundamentals are all matters of major concern. The content specialist is highly influential for the logical order he can bring to what is to be learned. Information is of greater significance than process, as indicated by the passive role of the learner and in the instruments that are used to judge learning.

It is hoped that in the eighties, reading instructors will heed the voices of Veblen, Carlyle, and the many others who suggest that superior instruction is concerned with the means, as well as the ends, of learning. We need to rediscover the learner and tolerate, indeed cherish, differences rather than conformity.

[7]Carlyle, Thomas. "Pedagogy" in *Unseen Harvests, A Treasury of Teaching.* New York: The Macmillan Co., 1947.

Learning needs to be viewed as an active enterprise, with children handling or working with processes rather than learning about them. When this is the case higher levels of literacy and higher scores on inferential comprehension tests can be achieved. Reading instruction would be characterized by such outcomes as the variety of books read, the reports written and given, as well as the typical test scores.

A second major implication of the National Assessment data for instruction is that the special attention given to populations that traditionally have difficulty with reading was beneficial and needs to be continued. These populations made the greatest gains over the decade. The special programs tend to be restricted to the primary grades, and while major gains are made at that level, some loss occurs over subsequent years as school becomes less and less attractive to these students. It is in this population that the major school dropout problem occurs. While well over 90 percent of the students complete high school in more favored situations, the dropout rate frequently exceeds 50 percent for minority students in large urban areas. It is this group that continues to add to the nation's functional illiteracy problem.

As suggested earlier, part of the problem of motivation in school is social and economic. However, the evidence is clear that these students can be motivated and can learn. Several schools have demonstrated this. Schools in the inner cities of New York, Chicago, Detroit, and elsewhere have achieved marked success with their students. The success of these schools and the educational activities of the sixties and seventies that opened the door of higher education for minority groups are beginning to have an important impact. These groups are becoming better integrated into society and are demanding more of their children and of the schools. Expectations have increased. In time this progress will decrease the school dropout and the adult illiteracy problems.

In the meantime, special programs need to be continued and extended to older age groups. New technology, in the form of microcomputers, word processors, and videodiscs bring the potential of freeing the teacher of much of the labor associated with individual diagnosis, prescription, and basic skills instruction. This can accomplish two major goals: that of providing highly individualized instruction and that of freeing teacher and student time to put skills to the kind of active use that leads to higher levels of performance.

The research of Ellson and Harris[8] can serve to emphasize the importance of such programs and as a caution of what the consequences might be if they are dropped. Working with children in twenty-three inner city schools in Indianapolis, they were able to increase the reading achievement of the bottom fourth of the students by 25 percentile points, and to reduce the number classified as mentally retarded and assigned to special education classes by two thirds. Their program, which is now in its eighteenth year, consists of fifteen minutes of structured individual instruction daily. During this time students are fully on tasks that lead to successful performance. The tragedy of not assisting such children in getting a good start in school is, all too often, that they become labeled as non-learners or mentally retarded, with expectations set accordingly.

Parents can play an important role in these programs as well. For her doctoral dissertation, Evelyn Mason has just completed an unusual evaluation of the Title One reading program in Indianapolis.[9] The evaluation is unusual in that she gathered qualitative information as well as quantitative data. The latter showed that the program met the traditional criteria for success. But Mason wanted to know what impact the Title One program had on the various people involved: parents, children, teachers, and principals.

The surveys and interviews with parents provided much useful information. The evaluation included grades 3–6 in thirty-three schools. Mason was concerned about relationships between parents and teachers, the nature of students' reading behavior at home, the students' attitudes about reading as perceived by their parents, the parents' knowledge of in-school activities, parent perceptions of program success, and the transfer value of the program into the home.

Ninety-three percent of the parents knew their children were in a special remedial program. The parents were impressed with their children's reading behavior outside of school.

---

[8]Ellson, Douglas G. and Phillip L. Harris. "Field Test of Programmed and Directed Tutoring," *Reading Research Quarterly*, Vol. 3, Spring 1968, pp. 307–67.

[9]Mason, Evelyn. *A Qualitative Analysis of the Impact of Remedial Reading on the Reading Achievement of Title I Students in the Indianapolis Public Schools.* Unpublished Doctoral Dissertation, Indiana University, 1981.

Eighty-seven percent reported that their children read at home (most at least twice a week). Seventy-seven percent believed their children's reading was very good to average; 88 percent of the children checked books out of the library; 82 percent reported that their children's reading increased after enrollment in the program; 84 percent reported their children liked the program. Mason concluded that the children were gaining skills in reading and were liking it more, and that the schools had solid support from the parents. Obviously, the program resulted in a high degree of interaction between parents and their children. The school encouraged an extensive parent involvement through pupil-parent learning packets and a contract that included the student, teacher, principal, and parent concerning reading at home. Mason concluded that there was an excellent transfer of positive pupil behavior into the homes and an increased positive attitude toward reading and toward themselves by the students. If success can become a style of living, these students are on their way both at home and at school.

Factors Related to Successful Reading Programs. A review of school reading programs soon reveals that some are more successful than others. Why this might be so has been studied in a variety of ways. Four years ago I undertook the task of gathering the opinions of teachers, reading specialists, and school administrators by personal interviews in their classrooms, schools and offices, and by questionnaires.[10] The schools and systems were selected by officials in state education departments because they were recognized for having effective programs. Both in the interviews and in the questionnaires my interest was to learn what the teachers and administrators thought were the most important factors leading to success or lack of reading achievement in their own school district.

Over a span of five months I visited twelve state departments of public instruction, thirty-six school districts, and more than 150 classroom teachers. Questionnaire data was gathered from an additional 51 schools and districts.

This effort was part of a larger study which included the collection and analysis of reading assessment data from 28 states. Among other factors the assessment reports were also analyzed to seek out what practitioners saw as enhancers or

[10]Fay, Leo. *Factors That Enhance Reading Achievement,* Paper presented at the International Reading Association Convention, Houston, May, 1978.

detractors to their success in teaching reading. From these various sources, four major impressions emerged:

1. Reading achievement is generally substantial and appears to be improving universally at the younger age levels and in an increasing number of places at higher ages (much the same as the National Assessment report).

2. The current basic skills and accountability emphasis may be misdirected, particularly if the emphasis is primarily upon the more mechanical skills of reading. Many teachers and administrators expressed concern that an overemphasis on basic skills would decrease the opportunity to develop higher levels of literacy and would thus depress higher levels of achievement. Many see the need for developing higher levels of competency as the most crucial need in American reading instruction. This attitude is in sharp contrast to the mandates in various states that school people and those concerned with reading generally must be more directly involved in the discussions and definitions underlying the basic skills and minimum competency movements.

3. Students who are not successful almost invariably have a history of never having been successful in their school reading experience. It is this small proportion of students who represent a major part of the so-called reading problem. *Pre-school and the beginning school experience are strikingly important and merit continued study and experimentation, including pre-school home involvement.*

4. The Right to Read effort has had a marked success in many states in developing a trained corps of leadership people in the schools. The importance of leadership for building strong programs was very apparent. Good practice does not just emerge. Invariably, good programs include strong leadership.

In the interviews and questionnaires, the respondents were asked to list those factors they considered important for enhancing reading instruction in their school, and those they thought detracted from their effectiveness. The results of the study are quite revealing in the importance attributed to affective factors, and in the lack of consistency in response to the factors that are often considered of prime consideration in improving instruction. The factors considered major enhancers were:

1. The teaching staff has a positive attitude toward teaching and their students ability to learn. Over 80 percent of the respondents listed this as a major enhancer. Often expressed was the idea that "Our school is a superior school because the teachers believe in what they are doing. They are positive people who enjoy teaching."
2. High expectations are set for success by school administrators; particularly by the principal, but also by the superintendent and the Board of Education.
3. Leadership is provided for reading program development and for in-service efforts at the school level. In most cases this leadership was provided by a reading specialist but not infrequently the principal was mentioned as the key person.
4. Good teacher-student relations prevail in the school.
5. Parents, students, and community react positively to and support the schools. Interestingly, newspapers and radio were frequently listed as community support, but in no case was television mentioned.
6. Parents and students have high expectations for achievement. Two states, Minnesota and Tennessee, assessed parent expectation as part of their assessment programs.

To the question, "What is the major detractor to successful reading instruction," several respondents said there were none. Responses were also more scattered than for the enhancers. However, three major detractors did surface:

1. Excessive television viewing that interfered with school work and kept students from reading. This was mentioned four times more often than the second item.
2. The lack of adequate fiscal support for materials, especially trade books, and for supportive programs—reading specialists, school psychologists, et al.
3. The lack of support from the home—particularly the lack of parents serving as positive models for reading.

Although different patterns of organizing for instruction, particular materials (usually a given basal reading program), and particular approaches had strong champions in a given school or district, no pattern of organization, specific material, or approach emerged as even a partial panacea for creating superior instructional programs. Also, although most research studies of reading achievement show a strong relationship between socioeconomic status and achievement, very few practitioners mentioned this as a positive or negative factor. Some very strong negative reaction was expressed concerning the role of teachers' associations and of the colleges and universities in pre-service and in-service training, or in other involvement in school practices. The strongest emotional reactions encountered—all negative—were in regard to the teachers associations and the colleges and universities.

Reading Instruction in the Electronic Age. During a discussion on public television concerning the impact of the rapid developments with computers, the narrator pointed to a microprocessor on the tip of his forefinger and predicted that this insignificant looking invention would cause a revolution more dramatic than the industrial revolution. The revolution, in fact, is well along and has reached the point where it is now having an impact upon school instruction. Two states, Minnesota and North Carolina, are well along in equipping all elementary and secondary schools with microcomputers for instructional purposes. Colleges and universities are busily engaged in developing computer literacy courses to be available for all students. For all concerned with the book, these developments are highly significant. For more than 500 years education and scholarship have been based upon the printed word. Now, as Sanders points out, we are faced with a rapidly evolving information technology that is shifting us away from print media as the primary source of information. The question is no longer whether computers are effective teaching tools, but rather how can education as we know it continue to meet the needs of society in a time when the information base is changing. Sanders concludes his discussion of this issue with the statement, "No challenge to our educational system has been any more dangerous than this which threatens to change both the content and the processes that serve as the very foundation of our educational programs."[11] The challenge is real but, perhaps, rather than dangerous, the new technology—the computers, word processors, and videodiscs—should be seen as means of gaining better control over the massive and growing amounts of information available.

The implications of this revolution for reading instruction

---

[11]Sanders, William. "Computers in Education: A Critical Challenge," *Viewpoints in Teaching and Learning,* Journal of the School of Education, Indiana University, Vol. 57, Spring 1981, pp. 129–133.

and for the keeping of school are still to be clearly defined, but the promise is great that education and reading will be prime benefactors. The software already developed for reading instruction is substantial and will soon increase markedly as the publishers of basal readers develop computer assisted materials to complement their print material.

Summary and Conclusion. In summary, the nation has largely met the goal of achieving basic, functional literacy for its citizens. The remaining problem for achieving total basic literacy relates primarily to those who do not complete high school. Important political, social, and economic as well as educational issues relate to the school dropout problem.

Primary among the educational issues is the need to realistically define literacy expectations for students with varying characteristics. Much of the criticism of the schools is based upon expectations that are not appropriate for many students.

For those who remain in school, the greatest apparent need is to achieve higher forms of literacy. The present emphasis on basic skills may be a negative force working against achieving higher performance levels.

The school cannot be totally effective working on its own. The home is an important source of support and a worthy complement to the school's instructional program. The school and the home can be mutually supportive in many ways, including that of setting high expectations for teachers and students.

As new developments take place in communications, the definition of literacy must once again be broadened. With television, literacy definitions were broadened to include visual literacy. Now, definitions need to be reworked to include computer literacy.

All in all, after one reviews what has been accomplished and reflects upon current developments, optimism is warranted for what reading will contribute to successful living.

ADDITIONAL REFERENCES

Cook, Wanda P. *Adult Literacy Education in the United States,* Newark, DE: International Reading Association, 1977.

Farr, Roger, Leo Fay and Harold H. Negley. *Then and Now: Reading Achievement in Indiana (1944–45 and 1976).* Bloomington, IN: School of Education, Indiana University, 1978.

Fay, Leo. "In Perspective," *Secondary Reading: Theory and Application*. Monograph in Languages and Reading Studies, School of Education, Indiana University, September, 1978, pp. 117–122.

Fay, Leo. *What is the Extent of Literacy in the United States?* Paper Presented at the National Council Teachers of English, November, 1980.

Hunter, Carman St. John and David Harman. *Adult Illiteracy in the United States.* New York: McGraw-Hill, 1979.

RESPONSES AND DISCUSSION

Leo Fay introduced discussion of his paper with the affirmation that we have established a phenomenal education base for our society, and that the schools have made a very positive contribution to this. At the time of the first United States census, the literacy level was comparable to that of people today living in Bangladesh and Pakistan. At the turn of the century only 2 percent of seventeen-year-olds actually graduated from high school; by the middle of the 1960s the figure was 75 percent. The question is, why do 25 percent leave without graduating? Research shows that, at present, 98 percent of the jobs in the United States have some literacy requirements, most of them falling between the tenth and twelfth-grade level. The labor force overall is functioning at this latter level, and demand will increase.

Again, we see the pendulum swinging to the back-to-basic emphasis, when in fact the need is to get beyond the basic skills. There must be more emphasis on reading to solve problems, and on reading that calls for critical thinking. No one in any field becomes a superior performer solely by learning skills. It is the application of skills in situations that require high levels of thought that makes for fine performance. As to technology, the computer has the capability of permitting and encouraging children to be creative. We should let them produce their own programs, using the word processing ability of the computer. We should encourage its use for problem solving and realize that all of this calls for a high level of reading ability. Education must counteract the forces of those who would censor and narrow curriculum. Learning to make choices is what education—and reading—is all about.

43

VIRGINIA MACY, *Chairman of the Education Commission of the National PTA*

First, it is a given, of course, that basic skills must be mastered and that signs of weakness require remediation. The question is: what can we do about the overemphasis in this area at the expense of a comprehensive reading program? All too often, minimum competencies are treated as maximums. We must be concerned, as Dr. Fay says, with inferential reading skills, and with the ability to become inquiring, critical thinkers. Yet because they want to be sure of getting good grades to get into college, college-bound students are counselled to take less meaty courses. Parents of every eighth-grader in California are sent a letter explaining what the minimum college entrance requirements are. High school students are being cut from six periods to five a day, and students are sometimes counselled to take as few as four periods per day for budget cutting purposes, as we continue to suffer from the cuts of Proposition 13. All this is not conducive to achieving literacy of the higher order.

What can be done? We need to explain to parents, to the press, and to the community at large, the shortcomings of the minimum competency testing approach at the expense of a comprehensive reading program. We need to reach into the home of every student to help parents understand the issue in its totality. The minimum competency campaign has been fanned by headlines and by often incomplete information and misinterpretation.

Dr. Fay has stated that, according to research, excessive television watching is mentioned far more often than any other factor as a deterrent to reading. This is substantiated by research in California, which shows that excessive television viewing leads to lower test scores. At the time they took their tests in the annual California Assessment Program, some 500,000 students were asked how many hours of television they watched. Test scores were inversely related to the amount of television watched: the more viewing the lower the test scores. Yet we know that television is a wonderful medium if used properly. The PTA is now changing the focus of its five-year-old television project from the industry's programming to the viewer, his habits, and skills. With the advent of so many channels and choices, the viewer must be taught to be selective and critical, and to think while he watches. The symposium held by the

Center for the Book was a landmark event. It spawned the development of viewing skills materials under a grant from the U. S. Department of Education. We would like to see viewing skills instruction taking place in every school and every home in this country. The classroom teacher can be trained to use television as a motivating tool to enhance student interest in reading.

Finally, I'd like to comment on ways of reaching parents, with any number of ideas, including those about reading. Isn't there some way we can reach the two breadwinner and single-parent families in the workplace? Couldn't we develop a set of topics of wide appeal relating to children's education—particularly reading—and secure some charismatic speakers who could go into the telephone company or the plant during lunch hours with short, important messages for people about their children? Conceivably, such sessions would motivate these parents to follow-up the ideas presented in their own schools. Parents who are adult learning models have a lot to do with motivation of children too.

MARILYN MILLER, *Associate Professor, School of Library Science, University of North Carolina at Chapel Hill.*

The community or the individual in pursuit of self-realization needs more than decoding or even comprehension from the reading instruction program. Knowing how to read, and applying those skills to the reading of books and other print material—whether newsprint, television, or computer monitor—both for personal growth and vocational necessity; and using the results of all that reading for personal enhancement, participation in government, and for attaining material security, makes reading equate with successful living.

Joyce Robinson, State Librarian of Jamaica, and director of Jamaica's literacy program, described her government's attack on illiteracy: "When we, in Jamaica, use the phrase 'functional literacy,' we are referring to the UNESCO definition, which refers to a person who is literate when he has acquired the essential knowledge and skills to enable him to engage in all those activities in which literacy is required for effective functioning in his group and community, and whose attainments in reading, writing, and arithmetic make it possible for him to use those skills toward his own and the community's development.

45

Reading directions and not needing to look at them again is not literacy. Reading to expand knowledge and experience is literacy."

When students on a university campus asked Maya Angelou, after her talk to a large audience, "What can we do to be survivors? How do we start?" she told them, "Literature, of course, is the answer. Go to the libraries. Read—read—read with a Catholic longing."

As superintendents, principals, reading teachers, and library media specialists work with parent support groups and other concerned citizens to achieve a higher level of literacy, we must articulate goals that speak both to instruction and beyond instruction, to the desire to read (motivation) and enjoyment in reading. *Decoding skills are basic tools, and comprehension can occur on many levels, but it is the desire to read and the enjoyment in reading that makes high-level literacy possible. George Canney at the University of Illinois notes, "For many reasons schools have tended to emphasize the first, wonder about the second, and all but ignore the latter two."*

Regardless of the goals and objectives the school community selects for its reading program, the teaching strategies should include role models who read. As Dr. Fay notes, learning needs to be viewed as an active enterprise in which children handle or work with processes rather than just learn about them abstractly. He goes on to note that reading instruction should be characterized by such outcomes as the variety of books read, the quality of the reports written and presented orally, as well as by the typical test scores. I would want to add to those characteristics inclusion of the research written after consulting; the investigation of numerous resource tools, both in print and audiovisual; and the art, music, dance, original stories, television programs, films, slide sets, and filmstrips produced and created in response to literature read and subject content area investigated.

Teaching strategies in reading must extend to the school's total curriculum and to its major teaching laboratory, the school library media center. Encouragement of reading must extend beyond the school to the public library, which is open during many non-school hours. It is difficult for many people, even educators, to grasp, without actually seeing it, how much learning takes place in the school library media center which is truly an integrated part of the instructional program. In a recent visit to a North Carolina school, I saw a fourth-grade class—the slowest academically in a school of 650 children—in their school library media center; the casual observer would never have recognized them as reluctant or retarded learners. They were reviewing with the librarian the information that belongs on a title page of a book, what a table of contents is, and how it is constructed. They had finished their work on reviewing the use of an index. Each student was investigating a natural disaster for a unit in earth sciences, and each was to produce a learning packet suitable for another student to use as a learning resource. The packets included a title page, table of contents, and a specified number of pages written in his or her own words. Among other items, students were to include a test for the peer user to evaluate his own learning, along with an evaluation form for the user to fill out evaluating the entire packet as feedback for the developer. Preparing all of this had involved the teacher, library media specialist, and volunteers, and resulted in much reading, comprehending, imagination, and motivation in both the classroom and the library media center.

Dr. Fay notes that the Title programs of the sixties and seventies have been effective in raising the reading scores of thousands of boys and girls. Those same title programs have provided millions of books, audiovisual equipment and materials, and have spurred the provision of excellent facilities in thousands of schools across this country for the use of these materials and for the production of learning materials. Additional materials are available in public libraries and together with some 60,000 school library media specialists there are hundreds of public librarians who are ready and able to be partners in the reading instruction program. Every week of the year hundreds of children's and young adult librarians in community libraries plan and carry out excellent programs which are aimed at making readers out of kids. The professional partners for the reading teacher and the classroom teacher are there, as are the materials; together they can face the challenge and the opportunity of the family-school partnership. Visual literacy instruction and parenting programs for the young are two of the activities that must be tackled as a team.

The computer has, of course, already caused a revolution, and there is more to come. *But remember: youngsters have to be able to read in order to interact with the computer.* The computer never gives up on people: it never gets a certain set to shoulders or face when a student misses the answer. It just gives him a cheery "Let's try again," or "Close, but read that last problem once more."

My electronics salesman tells me that the home will be the learning center of the future. His sales tell him so. I still equate what our Apple II does for me, when I use the script editor, with magic. It is phenomenal. But *we* buy the software; *we* can learn the program, and *we* can program children and young adults toward books, and toward research. *We* can provide simulations. *We* can provide access and processing assistance to information we have not yet dreamed of. It is *our* powerful arsenal of teaching tools. What we do with these tools will depend largely on how we plan together and share responsibility. *I do not believe that the schools are a service to the parents. I believe the schools are a service to the child and to the larger community.* In carrying out our responsibility to the *child* and to the larger community, we must help children to become literate in the broadest sense: to know how to read, to want to read, and to want to use the results of that reading for the betterment of society.

Comments from floor discussion. "I was glad to hear Marilyn Miller mention the role that volunteers can play in school library media centers, and to hear her review some of the groups of people who can be counted upon to work, inside and outside of the schools, on the development of high level literacy. I would like you to add to those in the community the members of Friends of Libraries, who now have their own national organization and are concerned with all libraries and reading. Members of Friends groups constitute a body of volunteers able to work on all of the kinds of things this group is concerned with." (Sandra Dolnik)

"If we develop critical reading skills, the critical viewing skills will come, because critical viewing comes from thinking, and reading *is* thinking. Kids know what's good when they are exposed to it, and brought into contact with it. Reading must be considered a form of civil defense." (Kenneth Komoski)

"We now have television children raising television children." (Virginia Macy) "And television teachers teaching them." (Nancy Larrick)

"Intervention must come early. The major inputs from television occur in children's prime language-learning years. It means that we have to do a lot of in-service training of teachers to relate viewing to reading. I have seen a project in Los Angeles in which children watch television with a teacher who stimulates the children to read books about the subjects in which television interests them. (Manya Ungar)

"We must recognize that reading is more work than watching television, but that in some schools there is a vestige of 'reading as chore.' "

"We must pay attention to the radical change that has taken place in the kinds of words children learn and use. There are whole categories of words—those having to do with outer-space or with drugs, for example—which were all but unknown to most of us twenty years ago, let alone to preschool children." (Carl Smith)

A Parent/Citizen's Perspective
Edward L. Palmer

(Dr. Edward L. Palmer has been the director of the Children's Television Workshop's research activities since CTW began in 1968. Previous to that he had completed, under the auspices of the Oregon State System of Higher Education, a federally-sponsored study of the attributes of television programs that most appealed to children between the ages of two and five. As a former member of the graduate faculty of Florida State University, he also carried out research on the thinking and learning processes of young children.

As vice president for research for CTW, he has designed and carried out numerous tests of television's effect on learning, advised other countries on adaptation of CTW's TV programs, and forged links and managed collaboration between commercial television producers and academic experts. He has been an associate in the Harvard University Center for Research in Children's Television since 1974, and is currently authoring a study of television for children in four cultures, the most recent of his many studies and articles on children and television.

Dr. Palmer received both his master's degree and his doctorate in the field of educational measurement and research design from Michigan State University in 1962 and 1964 respectively. In 1974 he received the American Psychological Association's annual award for Distinguished Contribution for Applications in Psychology.)

Writing from the perspective of a parent, I find myself relying as well upon my own background as a high school and college teacher, a reader and traveler, a researcher in early childhood education, and one who has devoted half a career to designing television programs for children. I draw from those experiences in making my first observation about the partner ship of home and school to promote reading in pursuit of successful living. Like William Shakespeare's character, I too find that ". . . one man in his time plays many parts. . . ." And in the many parts played by the many parents of our school children, there resides a resource which is incredibly rich, deep, and diverse. I see the nature of our question and our challenge

here as that of learning how to align all the many resources—
and the resourcefulness—of parents with those of the schools in
this endeavor, in such a way that all who participate personally
win.

I have been asked to address my comments especially to the
subject of motivation. In my view, the perception of personal
gain is fundamental in the motivational process, both in encouraging teachers and parents to collaborate, and in motivating
children to read. In addition to knowing from my own experience as a former teacher of high school English, I know as a
parent that teachers work hard, and I sense that to have their
hearts in an enterprise which involves extra costs in time and
effort, they will have to see pretty clearly from the outset how a
working partnership with parents can produce outcomes of the
sort they themselves are seeking. For parents, those who can
contribute time, talents, access to organizations, institutions, and
media, and in some cases even money, an opportunity to make
these resources available to promote reading by children in the
pursuit of successful living will be welcomed enthusiastically,
and in many cases backed up with substantial expenditures of
personal energies. In fact, for some portion of both the home
and school participants the task may consist of little more than
one of bringing the two together, facing them in the same
direction, and giving the signal to "forward, march." We know,
indeed, that out there in communities and school districts all
around the country, already the march is on, and, under one
banner or another, has long been in progress.

On the other hand, one of the problems with all partnerships is that they make demands. Not every parent will be
enthusiastic about this working partnership, any more than will
every teacher. Nor, for that matter, will all parents be willing or
able to rally to what may seem to us to be such a worthwhile
cause. Efforts to build effective home-school partnerships must
be reconciled to this reality, even while pressing for the widest
involvement possible. The inevitable fact that many parents
cannot be expected to participate concerns me very much, and
affects my role as a parent. In saying why, and how, and what I
think the issues and implications are in connection with this
entire home-school partnership, I will draw for a moment on
some statistics which I know about from my work with children
and television. My use of these statistics, by the way, is a concrete

illustration of my first point—which is that we parents do, indeed, have some specialized resources to bring to this home-school partnership. Most of these statistics come from recent reports of the Carnegie Commission on Children. I will use them to help communicate what I consider to be the problematic dimensions of the task of promoting reading in this country, as well as to provide overwhelming evidence of the need, and to challenge us all to maintain a comprehensive definition of what it is we are seeking to accomplish.

The number of children in the population under age fifteen has dropped since 1970, by about 25 percent. In the meantime, the twenty-five to thirty-four-year olds and those sixty-five and older have increased by approximately 30 percent and 20 percent, respectively. What this means, according to some interpretations, is that as adults, today's shrunken population of children will have to provide the nation's productive force, support an enormous number of the elderly, and, at the same time, rear their own children. Moreover, with proportionately higher fertility rates among minority groups, a much greater portion of this productive force will be recruited from predominately low-income, urban populations. But this is only a part of the reality drawn so vividly by the statistics on children. While assuring us that most of today's young children will grow up to be "strong and capable, healthy and whole adults," the president of Carnegie Corporation, Alan Pifer, in a recent foundation report, cites the following sobering facts:

> Nationally, three million arrests were made for juvenile crimes last year; millions of children suffer from drug and alcohol abuse; one million teenage girls become pregnant each year; a million youngsters run away from home; suicide has become the highest killer of teenagers after accidents. We know that the abuse and neglect of children have reached shocking proportions, that hundreds of thousands of children lead miserable lives in institutions, that millions are physically, mentally, or emotionally disabled, that half a million are in foster care, that well over a million under the age of fifteen are not in school, that the national school drop-out rate is 15 percent, and that upwards of 500,000 children age sixteen and under, most of them from

migrant families, are working in the fields because of loopholes in the child labor laws, while the real unemployment rate for urban black youths is believed to be over 50 percent.

An irony is that public attitudes toward the plight of children are unresponsive, and in many cases antagonistic, and that our nation is experiencing what Pifer cites as "the collapse of the child's cause."

The figures presented by Mr. Pifer are profoundly distressing. Yet their meaning is made only more drastic in light of the increasing stresses on the family, the current tendency toward withdrawal and self-centeredness among adults, and the reluctance at the local or federal levels to support education adequately.

These are our children and the peers of our children. They will grow up together and take on the responsibilities of life and of running our nation together, and the quality of life of each, in enjoyment or in pain, inexorably will seep through and affect the quality of life enjoyed by all the others. I firmly believe there are parents who can help reach these children, where often their own parents cannot; some parents who, given the chance, will want to help, and perhaps some who won't. How are those who, like their predecessors throughout history, have the ability to help children, to be enlisted in helping to nurture more than just their own? I don't presume to have the answer, but I'm convinced it must be large in the agenda for this home-school partnership.

This brings me to the next point about the home-school partnership, which is that in our joint endeavor to motivate children's reading, we are by no means faced with anything quite so fundamental as inventing the first wheel. Without having attempted a systematic survey of existing practices, I know, as an interested parent, that out there already in the schools across the nation are teachers, librarians, school administrators, and counselors who are exercising great imagination and skill in exciting children about books and reading. And while this business of strengthening the link between home and school as a major programmatic thrust is perhaps new for us all, the existence of local initiatives, such as the Foxfire Experiment, can help to remind us that natural models already exist. As a parent attempting to collaborate with the schools, especially as a working parent, I wouldn't care to do the original research involved in locating all the successful efforts to motivate these children or those, from this home environment or that, through one form of parental participation or another (or even, in some cases, in spite of none), to read or to write . . . but I certainly would welcome a chance to hear about ongoing efforts that seem to work well, and to hear some opinions on why they do work, and how to emulate their successes.

I have alluded to parents who already are effective in motivating their children's reading, and to those who for one reason or other never will or could be. Inbetween is a large group of parents who can and will join in, given the proper conditions and encouragement. In order to prompt their participation, we need to know as much as possible about their characteristics. This large, important group probably do not very regularly attend school functions unless their children are very young. Most, including both men and women, are employed full or part-time outside the home. Their children watch upwards of four hours of television every day, much of it more adult than child-oriented fare. All are experiencing the economic pinch, some due to inflation, high interest rates, the high cost of housing; others, due to lack of jobs. Many are adjusting to the idea of living with less in the way of material goods and comforts than their parents enjoyed. The dream of progress—of an ever-expanding economy, and of ever-expanding futures for our children—is either not being talked about much or is being talked of as outmoded in modern American life. In their great diversity, these parents themselves reflect the gamut of human situations.

I have dwelt on problems, because they reflect the harvest of our misplaced values, of circumstance, and of little understood forms of human frailty. They all reduce the needs of the spirit, needs to which books can help bring solutions and constructive, even if sometimes only soothing, perspectives. But there also are the higher callings of art and science and spirituality, and skills of ordinary, practical living, to be advanced through reading.

Preplanning Issues. As a parent, I would like to have available clear and precise information about the various uses of books in the lives of children, as well as tips about how to put this information into practice. Moreover, if there is to be a home-school partnership, I expect the school to provide the impetus for launching it, and to be clear, before involving me, about the firmness of and purpose for its own commitment. I expect the school to have assembled a sufficient amount of background material to at least launch the collaborative process, whether this is initially to be in the form of basic planning or will consist of moving directly into activities. I would like to be assured that the school is clear or seeking to become clear for itself about the special advantages that are expected to result from the home-school partnership. I am sure this is something which will become clearer to both sides through the actual process of collaboration itself, and yet, certainly for many parents, the idea could die aborning if we have to wait overly long between the first meeting and the time when the collaboration and its work-ings begin to take on some clear shape. On the school side of the partnership, there are enormous real or potential resources: trained classroom and library professionals, libraries them-selves, access to literature about children and books, and na-tional organizations to provide research, planning, models, and materials of various sorts. We parents need to be concerned about the availability of funds to mobilize and support us in making use of these resources.

What system is there or will there be for allowing parents to express their questions and ideas and desires about the direc-tions and activities of the home-school partnership? Can I ask a question and get an answer? Or can there be available a compen-dium of questions most often asked by parents like me, along with answers? Who can I ask for help if my child of normal intelligence has not yet mastered reading by grade four, and if, moreover, the school seems stymied as to why and is at a loss as to what can be done? How can I help make books compete with the television? One of my acquaintances claims book reading can increase children's intelligence, and I want to know whether or not this is true, and if true, which books to acquire, and where. What are the answers?

Questions like these may be useful to consider at this stage because of the other questions they raise in turn. What materials are needed to serve this home-school partnership? Who finds this out? How are such efforts coordinated efficiently so experi-ences can be shared? What will be the nature and limits of the school's role? Will the schools play the funneling and coordinating role between national organizations and parents or local parent organizations? Do schools want to play such a role? Are they prepared to financially? What are the costs?

Some broad questions of program and strategy also need to be answered at the preliminary stage. For instance, we can ask what minimum use of existing staff and facilities are required to establish and sustain an on-going home-school partnership? What new priority expenditures at the national level would contribute the most to the support of the home-school partnership with reasonable cost? What societal benefits will result when parents and schools are involved in a workable home-school partnership—e.g., in terms of greater parental support for schools, increased national productivity, and improved family cohesiveness? And what is the measure of the loss in cases in which individual schools and individual parents participate briefly and then drop out? Do school personnel in key positions possess the resources, the organizational and interpersonal skills, and the level of interest required to make the partnership work? Can the kinds of support and materials they need be made available in simple, accessible, and inexpensive yet effective form? Are any special steps required to coordinate this particular home-school activity with other programs in the already on-going home-school partnership? How big and expensive an enterprise are we talking about, and how is that decided? What will be the balance of centralized, relative to local, grassroots activity? What do we know about helping grassroots efforts to get started and grow? Are there models of successful home-school partnerships, community wide, initiated at the grassroots level, whose approach and program could be disseminated? Going still further are there models of successful dissemination? Can there be continuity through the grades so I as a parent can learn how best to approach my child in light of developmental level?

Motivation of Action Steps. Some of our best lessons about motivation come from literature. Tom Sawyer, for example, exhibited a precocious sagacity about this aspect of human nature in understanding that his peers actually would trade items of value in return for the opportunity to help whitewash his fence. We might take a page from his book in looking to the purposes of the home-school partnership. I noted earlier that people who also happen to be parents have access to an enormous range of useful resources. Any home-school group can appropriate various community resources for the purpose of extending its effectiveness. In doing so, it can count on the willing participation of many individuals and organizations. It would be a challenge as a parent to sit with other parents and school personnel and attempt to take inventory of such opportunities. Given the idea and the opportunity, this kind of activity is one in which many parents would participate willingly, and it is one which moves in the direction of reaching out to other parents, and to those children who perhaps otherwise would not be reached.

Many people will contribute resources for many reasons, but a useful tip for local home-school organizations is to look for situations in which the contributor's cause is advanced by making the contribution. Newspapers, for instance, want to motivate youth to acquire the newspaper-reading habit, and in addition, will often announce and otherwise promote community projects. Large numbers of volunteer organizations, especially those involved in health and safety, are eager to reach children with their messages, and of course there is a great deal of room for other forms of volunteering. Traditions already exist in reading to the blind, the operation of book tables and participation in book fairs, to mention only a few. It would also be useful to read orally to children who are experiencing difficulty in learning to read, to reluctant readers, and to children who are mentally disabled or emotionally disturbed.

Tips directed to parents on promotion of reading, made available on a regular, periodic basis, can accomplish a great deal, especially if the ideas are do-able within the means and convenience of most parents. A monthly tip sheet, for instance, would not only serve as a useful periodic reminder, but could also constitute a type of minimal vehicle for establishing home-school collaboration; perhaps it would also promote active participation on the part of parents who lack the time or inclination to actually attend conferences. The tips need not be elaborate. One example is to provide an atmosphere of respect for the requirements of someone who is reading. An explanation of the importance of storytelling in the motivation of reading interest is another. Others are reminders to read occasionally to children who are experiencing reading difficulty, without demanding that they participate in the reading or learn specific reading skills. Other tips could include: book choices, geared to different interests and developmental levels; qualities to look for in buying children's books (e.g., what the Newbery and Caldecott medals look like, and what they mean); the suggestion that parents make a point of reading some of the books their children are reading, to establish points of contact and to help parents and children discover the many gratifications of shared literary experiences; the suggestion that the television be shut off for a period of time each day in favor of a family reading period; the suggestion of reading an extended book aloud, by daily installments, along with one's children, accompanied by discussion; the suggestion of helping children to explore different worlds and values and experience different benefits through reading—ranging from the lyricism of poetry to the amazing intricacy and variety of forms in the natural world, to the power of ideals and of love and friendship; including access through books to activities, to the exploits of others, and to writings on the lifestyles of different people and the history of peoples and of other living things, to the wonders and instruments of the man-made world; and of course, the idea of letting your children read to you.

There are many other simple and easy things parents can be encouraged to do. For example, seeing that children are occasionally exposed to a given work at different stages in their development; giving books as gifts; watching for ways to support children's differences when their tastes and book habits turn out to be different; discussing books with children to help develop taste, critical judgment, and a healthy skepticism about the validity of assertions which happen to appear in print; and the idea of using books to trigger discussion when sensitive subjects come up, such as an experience by the child of personal failure, the need for either the parent or the child to go to the hospital, the arrival of a new sibling, or specific occasions involving fears or apprehensions; the value of providing children with the opportunity to read different books by the same author, and of letting them know who wrote a particular book, and when, and what the name of the illustrator is; and letting children have and trust their own feelings about a book.

It is always important to provide incentives, and one of the most effective in any domain of activity is to have a clearly defined, valued goal, or set of goals or purposes. Goals as incentives come into play when we identify the various functions reading can serve with children. Each function identified can be stated as a goal, and there can be subsidiary goals, in turn. There is incentive value when the goal is stated not broadly as that of encouraging one's child to read, but precisely, as encouraging the child to relax and enjoy some simple good humor, or to read about areas of career opportunity, or learn to ski, build a hut in the woods, make a pie, or to engage some particular moral dilemma. There is value in knowing about different goals, *a priori*, so book choices can be made to advance them, and there is value in knowing what objectives a specific book can help to fulfill.

Tips such as these will be more effective, in my opinion, if they are presented not merely as activities, but as activities to be undertaken in pursuit of clearly articulated objectives. Even if the goals seem clear by implication, it can be useful to state them. I am referring here, for example, to the added motivational value of stating for the parent the specific purposes sought in exposing children at different stages in their development to the same book, and the specific kinds of outcomes achievable through reading in the area of career possibilities. To illustrate, goals for parents in guiding children's reading about careers would include helping their children: (1) to learn about the place of one's work in one's life; (2) to explore their own personal qualities, and the relation of these to aspects of different careers, (3) to be deliberate in making career (and other) choices, and (4) to begin early to prepare themselves with essential career prerequisites. An extended set of goals of this sort, in addition to providing motivation and giving focus to our efforts, would go a long way toward creating a more precise definition of "reading in the pursuit of successful living."

The metaphors brought to the home-school partnership by the various participants play a powerful motivational role. To illustrate, just imagine the contrast in effectiveness for the teacher who approaches the partnership with an image in which each participant is "supposed" to go half-way, as compared with one who is prepared to go 100 percent of the way. Not every school participant will be prepared, either by constitution or philosophy, to make the extent of effort needed to reach the hard-to-reach parent. Accordingly, perhaps there should be a "100 percent Club" for those who are.

Other important qualities of the working partnership, and

of the entire enterprise, will also be approached by participants according to either a more or less productive metaphor, or image. To attempt to reach reluctant parents can be viewed as giving them more than they deserve, an uphill battle, a losing cause, or as an activity outside one's training and job description, and therefore, outside one's purview; or else it can be viewed as a problem we've all lived with for too long and to which we need some answers, an occasion for overcoming indifference transmitted down through generations, a constructive response to the stresses of contemporary family life, or an obligation to give every child a vision of the successful life, and the wherewithal through books to broaden and pursue that vision.

Participants in this partnership who think in terms of sitting on the same side of the problem facing it side by side will make a qualitatively different contribution than those who conceive of themselves as sitting at loggerheads. Those who think of linking up forces which are already moving or are inclined to move in the same direction will have more successes than those who don't. Those who think in terms of providing an occasion for people to choose so they can be given what they themselves say they want will be more effective promoters than those who only come full of advice. Those who come prepared to deal with categories of children will be less effective than those prepared to achieve something appropriate for each child, without regard for such labels as rich/poor (the rich child may be book poor), gifted/learning disabled, good reader/poor reader. Those prepared to let a child read or be read to from a book far above that child's head when that is what the child wants will be more successful than one whose otherwise valid ideas about the developmental suitability of different books are applied in ways which are rigid and inflexible. The teacher or librarian who is willing to collaborate with parents by correspondence, and not exclusively face to face, will achieve a wider outreach, and in the process will eventually achieve more face-to-face interaction. The teacher prepared to deal with individual differences in parents—just as must be done with children—will enjoy the process more and be more effective. The school staffer who is prepared to take advantage of the specialized skills and resources parents can bring to the partnership will be more successful than one who tries to do the whole job alone. The participant who is prepared for the value and forms of participation to evolve from the process of participation itself will experience more of the gratifications of creating than will one who wants everything spelled out by someone else in advance. All these preconceptions will need to be considered in designing the symbols and images of the partnership, and in framing descriptions of roles, goals, and processes.

School personnel bring years of special professional training and experience to the awesome process of nourishing the intellectual growth of children. We parents are in great need of their guidance in helping each of us to find a collaborative role we will find comfortable and gratifying. I am convinced that as a group, we parents can do more and want to.

RESPONSES AND DISCUSSION

Edward Palmer introduced discussion of his paper by expressing his belief that people like options. Parents will participate in matters relating to their children and to learning by self-selection rather than by assignment, but they need encouragement and training to do this. Motivation includes giving people a chance to help complete a plan or a project—to put something of themselves into it. "An open gestalt longs for closure," said Ed Palmer, so the big job is to open possibilities and channels through which people can bring to closure what they set out to do, through their own efforts. Motivation, Palmer suggested, means providing a channel through which the natural tendency of the flow can be facilitated. Being well-educated has a lot to do with motivation; families have to be motivated themselves in order to be able to motivate children. This idea refers once again to adult models who read books: the best advertisement for reading is seeing people read, which holds true for any habit.

It is important to involve in this, as in other aspects of motivation, the parents-once-removed: the grandparents. Politically speaking, grandparents and children are in competition, yet grandparents are the natural allies of children. There must be an atmosphere of respect for persons who are engaged in reading, and who have read a lot and can share what they have read. There must be an understanding of the importance of storytelling to reading. And it is important to read aloud to children who are experiencing difficulty in reading, without demanding that they give back evidence of having acquired reading skill. *Discussing what is in books is important to help develop taste and critical judgement.* It is useful for many reasons to introduce books as part of the discussion of sensitive subjects such as divorce, death or sex.

Finally, we probably need to bring more marketing talent to bear on books and reading. This is a marketing-oriented society; people, even children, are used to being sold things. They are used to being persuaded. Perhaps we need more posters and bumper stickers everywhere, with funny messages, messages that attract attention:

"A Book in Time Saves a Stitch," "Old MacDonald Had a Book," or "A Book a Day Keeps the Doctor Away."

LUCILLE C. THOMAS, *Assistant Director for Elementary Schools, Office of Library Media and Telecommunications, New York City Board of Education*

We must remember that "education" and "school" are not synonymous. Everything a child learns in school and out of it is truly learning, and the principle that Whitman expressed so well in his poem still stands: *That which the child experiences becomes a part of him.* It is a given that parent involvement enables a child to achieve better and to learn more. The more the teacher knows about the child, the better the teacher will understand and be able to help him. Parents help by sharing what they know and understand about their child. Parents need to be given an awareness, a basic understanding about reading, an understanding that it supplies a channel through which a child's interests can flow and be expanded. They *need to be aware that reading is not a process of getting meaning from the page, but that symbols awaken meaning which is already in the mind of the reader, meaning that has been put there by past experiences.* Parents of young children must be made aware that much of what is involved in reading readiness takes place even before the child enters kindergarten. Perhaps we must get involved with expectant parents and with the increasing numbers of programs about parenting. Parents are never as anxious to do right by their baby as they are during the prenatal period, so they should learn to expect, and be trained for, setting time aside for reading as part of the prenatal training package.

Parents must learn that acquiring basic reading skills will not create readers unless those skills are used, and grow as the

62

child grows. It is essential that when building the home-school partnership, that family strengths, and not deficits be reinforced. This approach magnifies and builds upon the assets inherent in the family. It draws upon the family's resources and abilities to reinforce what the school may be doing with reading.

The non-deficit approach is based upon the belief that all children have some meaningful experiences upon which reading comprehension and interests can be built. We need to try to see these experiences in terms of their meaning and importance to a child. On our way here today, our taxi driver told us how his father and he shared the experience of watching the United States presidents pass by their home on the way to Andrews Air Force Base. When he told his teacher about this, the teacher projected a negative attitude and thought that he was making things up, to the extent of sending a letter home complaining that the child was imagining seeing important people. But the man still remembers the father's influence on his learning, and the sharing of experiences.

All parents possess intrinsic abilities to help their children learn, and concern can be translated into practical support for children and for the school experience. There are some considerations which may serve as guidelines in developing a 'parents-are-partners' program: (1) Parent participation is most widespread and sustained if a parent realizes the link to achievement. We need to make people aware that 98 percent of jobs require some degree of reading, and that if a child is able to read well his chances of getting a better job are greater; (2) The quality of life is improved if you are able to read fluently. This must be conveyed to parents in terms they understand and can relate to.

Don't ever feel that inner city or poor parents are not interested. They may not have much education or training, but they are anxious to help their children. It is up to us to let them know in a very clear way how they can help.

There should be a parent corner, and a day when parents can come to the school library. Its basic philosophy, objectives, and role expectations, should be well defined. We have tried "living room seminars," in which parents who live in the same building or on the same block form groups or clusters and decide on topics to talk about—for our purposes, reading. Each member of the cluster takes a turn serving as host or hostess to a small group. It is quite effective, and reaches those parents who might not come to a meeting at the school or elsewhere away from home ground.

Send home a reading recipe with children—some books to read and talk about—with follow up activity. Add some books that older children can read aloud to younger brothers and sisters.

It is important to realize that books can actually help children to overcome some of the barriers presented to them by handicaps. Dorothy Butler, author of *Cushla and Her Books* (see suggested readings) says: "I know now what print and pictures have to offer a child cut off from the world for whatever reason, but I know also that there must be another human being prepared to intercede before anything good can happen." The message is clear to all of us who are concerned for the development of all children: *We must accelerate the recruitment of human links between books and children.* The school is the one social institution that has contact with students over time; it has the opportunity and the responsibility to reach out to the students' families and involve them in this most important step toward successful living.

WILMER S. CODY, *Superintendent, Birmingham, Alabama Public Schools*

I have to say that in my experience much of the perceived intimidation of parents by the schools is in the eye of the beholder, but if it is true that some parents feel intimidated by some teachers in some schools, I believe that there is something that can be done about it.

When I arrived in Birmingham, I discovered that in some of the schools, homework was no longer assigned. I met with the faculty of a particular school where this came to my attention, and I asked why not? They said, "Well, kids won't do it anymore." I asked why they would not do it anymore. They said, "Well, the parents won't make them do it." When I asked why this was the case, they said, "Well, the parents just don't care." I thought there was something very wrong with that because I had talked with enough parents to know that I had never met a parent who didn't care. There are parents with lots of personal problems who get very preoccupied with them, and I've known parents and single parents who have to work and who have heavy demands on their time. I've met parents who get so frustrated with personal or financial conflicts or their own limitations that they seem not to have time and attention to give, but I don't believe I have ever met a parent who did not really want to do something to help his or her child. There are a few exceptions out there, of course—we have mentally disturbed parents associated with our schools, too—but parents not caring is just not a legitimate generalization. However, one of the problems we face—at least in urban school systems—which calls for a practical solution, is that this false generalization is planted firmly in the minds of many classroom teachers, and principals, too. It is often born of their own frustration and inability to fill the demands of roles as we perceive them.

Therefore, one of the things we have to face in terms of a solution is a modification of our roles and responsibilities, and more specifically, the way in which we allocate our time. When we talk of teachers doing more, or of more teachers doing more to involve parents in engaging their children in activities that would help them to read, we are really talking about both parents and teachers changing the way in which they perceive their roles. We are competing with other role expectations held by classroom teachers, principals, and parents. Financial cutbacks might actually be turned to our advantage once we get past the point of thinking of them as devastating. Instead, we must try to think of how we can do something important that actually doesn't require much money: maximize the greatest resource that the school system has, which is the time of the classroom teacher. Indeed, eighty-five percent of our budget goes to personnel. This is a far greater percentage than the amount of our Title I money, which constitutes only 8 percent of our budget.

When I went to Birmingham, there were five teachers, working with approximately ten parents each, in a parent education program. I was excited about the program as a way to reach into the homes of preschool children. Each of the homes was visited weekly. Special materials were taken along, and parents were helped to undestand and learn what they could do to help their children learn. Beautiful. The materials were really nice. But—fifty sets of parents and five teachers when the district had 4,000 kindergarten or five year olds? The parents were self-selected: those who came forward and asked to get into the program comprised the group. Why, I asked, didn't we just go and pick some parents whose problems we thought might be most severe? The answer I received was, "Our program might then not succeed." Well, we had to make a change. We had to look at how we could serve all of the preschool children and their parents (we now have 5,000 children). We couldn't possibly afford to extend the program as it was operating, so we developed a different kind of program that would involve more parents. Our teachers, and also the parents, had to modify both their roles and their perceptions of them. We now have special clinics and workshops in the schools directed by regular classroom teachers along with brief and practical one-sheet flyers that go home, suggesting things to do with your child this week. I know we are not reaching all 5,000 children, but we are reaching out to many more than before. We are moving from rhetoric to action, from pilot or demonstration to real impact.

A plan is needed to spur action—a plan for the classroom, for the school, and for the school system. It must be a plan which recognizes that all parents are not alike in what they are able and willing to do. It should include some specifics and some alternatives, and some choices for parents to make—but very specific choices, in terms of activities. Expectations should be reasonable. We had a handbook of twenty-five or thirty pages describing what parents could do, and it was just too much—some parents just couldn't get beyond the first page. We had a series of workshops in which we semed to be trying to turn parents into teachers. We have had to modify our plans, and to consider what people are capable of doing.

Most important, such a program needs to reach a greater proportion of the community. We need to get beyond the idealized pilot program and implement on a large scale. The plans need to keep being reinforced or revised by the action taken. We also need to have meetings with parents, to praise them and to share their activities, and pride, in their achievements. We even need to give out rewards—a handmade pillow has been especially popular and appreciated. It's all quite similar to what we do with the children in terms of reward and reinforcement. I am not so sure that the parents—or ourselves for that matter—are so very different from the children, and it might be helpful on occasion to remember that.

Parents will respond to suggestions about what to do with their child if it is possible, i.e., reasonable in extent and satisfying to them and their child. Schools can effectively tap this major resource—parents in partnership with schools.

THOMAS P. FITZGERALD, *Supervisor, Basic Skills, The State Education Department, University of the State of New York*
Four major observations discussed in this paper struck a responsive chord. First, the staff in our schools should make a greater effort to publicize schools' goals, objectives, and expectations. This would generate broader support from parents. Second, a "tip sheet" should be initiated to provide direction and motivation for parents working with the children. Parents are eager to help their children to learn, if the parent feels capable. Third, most parents acknowledge the expertise of teachers, but feel we are spending more tax dollars on education than are necessary. Fourth, too many parents abdicate their role in educating their children. As a result, when parent committees are formed, few are willing to give their time to activities that take place within the school building.

From my point of view, greater emphasis should be placed on the cooperative roles played by the three agents charged with the responsibility for education: children, parents and teachers. Such cooperation is the basis for any home/school partnership. Consider for a moment the competency testing program used in various states. Whether you approve or disapprove of such programs, one positive outcome of the use of such tests is that the roles of each of these three agents is now more clearly delineated.

Dr. Palmer commented that there is an erosion of faith in our schools. We should remember that this is caused in part by our broadened perception of learning: we now know that all learning does not take place within school walls, and we recognize the contributions of parents and communities to the education of children. We know that many knowledge absolutes are subject to change, as well.

What seems to be needed is dialogue. Parents should be encouraged to describe their aspirations for their children. There is a need too, to articulate school programs within the community. Administrators should do some revamping of their roles to emphasize comprehensive planning and public information, and documentation of successful home/school programs should be publicized.

In developing a more extensive and functional home/school partnership, consideration should be given to what we know about children who are able to perform well both in and out of school. These youngsters have several characteristics: extensive background of experiences, extensive concept development, and extensive vocabulary. Their command of language enables them to demonstrate and express knowledge. They also have highly developed listening and speaking skills. Such children are successful in developing a positive self-concept. These characteristics, developed in all children, should be the goal of our partnership.

Parents should be encouraged to produce psychologically comfortable homes, to participate in a home/school partnership, and to contribute their time to children for the development of communication skills. Children should be encouraged to think, to communicate, and to expend an effort in learning. Teachers should recognize the partners they have in parents, assist them in reinforcing learning, and stay in communication with them. Administrators should build a climate for this through a network of school/community relations, study committees, and feedback channels for parents.

Most essential, parents and teachers should consciously model what reading can mean in peoples' lives. Adults must explain why they read, and what one can expect to get out of reading. We must help parents and teachers to be aware of some simple effective things that they can do to encourage reading, and suggest how to do them. Children don't always get out of experiences exactly what we expect them to get; experiences must be followed up in terms of their perceptions of what they saw, heard or did, and not only the perceptions that we think they should have had. We would raise anxieties in some parents if we expected them to teach their children, and we must not ask parents to learn techniques that are complicated or that appear phony or fatuous.

I close here with an illustration drawn from personal experience. I decided to try to share some books with my young daughter. We were to ask each other two questions about the books we had read. She saw through my technique and decided to trick me; the teacher-ish vehicle broke down, but she was willing to go along with my intent, so we had a good free-flowing discussion about the books instead, and were content.

If we could just get every parent to feel comfortable in being able to discuss things with his child, and to feel confident that this reinforces what the school does and that the school values and needs this reinforcement, we could achieve everything this meeting is about.

Comments from floor discussion. I would summarize so much of what has been said here, and underscore it, by saying: we have not one curriculum but several curricula in our schools. We have an *official* curriculum in which we focus upon skills; we have an *extra* curriculum, through which we teach in the affective domain (things having to do with character and values) in which parents are incredibly powerful teachers; we have the *hidden* curriculum—the rules and expectations of all concerned with education, which lie beneath the surface; and we have the *required* curriculum, which is what kids have to do and learn to "pass" to be "successful," whatever they may think or feel or whatever they may or may not have learned. We simply cannot expect most parents to be the teachers of the official curriculum.

One danger of overly specifying goals with minimum competency testing and such, is that many people will overreact to the necessity of meeting those required goals to the point where they lose track of the larger and more important goals. What we test, what we measure, and how we demand outcome products from children tends to narrow definitions of learning, and interferes, for example, in reading by children for the sheer enjoyment of it. We must do something positive to prevent the overly-narrow structuring of the curriculum. (Paul Salmon)

A Library Media Specialist's Perspective
Peggy Sullivan

(Dr. Peggy Sullivan is Dean of the College of Professional Studies at Northern Illinois University, a position she accepted in 1981. Immediately before going to DeKalb, she had served as Assistant Commissioner for Extension Services at the Chicago Public Library, following a career as a children's librarian, a school library media specialist, a planner and administrator of library projects, and a library school professor. As Director of the Knapp School Libraries Project in 1963– 68, Dr. Sullivan served her first tour of duty at the headquarters of the American Library Association. Travelling the country, to meet with educators, librarians, parents, and other citizens, to encourage and evaluate the demonstration projects, she learned much of what the public expects and hopes for the schools and the education of children.

As UNESCO consultant on school libraries, Dr. Sullivan visited Australia in 1970. She has held part-time faculty appointments at several library schools; provided technical assistance to films about libraries, and served as president of the American Library Association in 1980–81.

Dr. Sullivan received her master's degree in Library Science from the Catholic University of America in 1953, and her doctorate from the University of Chicago in 1972. She is eminently qualified to represent the views and perspectives of the library media specialist regarding the family-school partnership for reading and successful living. A version of this paper appeared as an article in School Library Journal, February, 1982.)

Exploring the many facets of the theme, "Reading and Successful Living," is an experience which encourages nostalgia, reminiscence, thoughtful interviewing of others, and, of course, reading. The relationships between reading and successful living are many. Most of us who consider ourselves real readers seldom think of reading as a tool, but it certainly is that. We appreciate tools most when a new environment or a new need calls our attention to those we take for granted in everyday life.

I have just recently moved to a new home and a new job, so

my appreciation for tools is at a higher level than usual. Getting a good pair of scissors permanently located in a convenient drawer and remembering which drawer is an effort, but it is well worth it because I recognize the need for that tool in a new setting. Similarly, adjusting to a new supermarket, a new bank, and a new hardware store made me appreciate the taken-for-granted values of being able to read and to respond to the signs, the directions, and the labels which, in a few weeks, I will hardly notice as I go about my business.

As I was choosing some cotton yarn to use for new hotpads for my new kitchen, I read through some directions for knitting and crocheting in the local dime store. I have always been supercilious about people who use the same patterns over and over when there is such a rich variety in pattern-books. Standing there in the store with the book in my hand, I remembered the first Monday after I had learned to knit. To use the phrase my family uses, I had learned to knit on a Friday evening, and I had "knitted up a storm" over the weekend, going to my aunt for further instructions every time I came to a place where I needed to do something different. Panic hit me when it was time for my aunt to go to work on Monday, and I said, "But what will I do if I want to go on knitting?" Very reasonably, she answered, "As long as you can read, you ought to be able to do anything!" And she handed me the instruction book and left. With that assurance, I was able to be independent.

People who write and speak about their early experiences with reading fall into two distinct groups. Those who emphasize its joys and pleasures tend to overlook its usefulness as a tool for the day-to-day business of successful living. Mary Ellen Chase, Clifton Fadiman, Bennett Cerf, among others, have expressed their own pleasures in reading and have shown how a commitment to reading has been a significant part of their lives. A major quarrel I have with them is that they tend to forget, or perhaps to be unaware of, what it is like not to read, not to recognize reading as a pleasure. People in this group, for example, say things like, "It doesn't make any difference what you read. Just keep reading!"

Like these dedicated readers, I read the sides of cereal boxes, the old ordinances posted in hotel rooms, and the almost illegible tiny print that comes wrapped around medicine bottles. But I am always aware that this kind of reading differs from the reading that gives insight to other people's minds and that provides beauty which is in itself satisfying. At the other end of the spectrum are the people who write and talk about reading as though it is *only* a tool. They stress it as a skill, but they seem to forget that it should accomplish something for us, that life should be better even as we learn to take it for granted as a tool; and that we should find in the tool itself much satisfaction. It is essential that some part of our society should be concerned with the techniques of reading; warning us when and why Johnny can't read, and providing the research and the know-how to spread the ability to read. But this group of people needs to be reminded that reading should give pleasure, and that somewhere along the line, the same children who have to be taught to "attack" words in learning to read should have the opportunity to learn to love the words they are attacking.

There is an even more annoying category of adults who do some disservice to the idea of reading and the part it plays in successful living. This consists of those who have mastered the skill and who may, in fact, do some secret reading for pleasure. But they are reluctant to admit that their busy, successful lives allow them time for reading as a pleasure in itself. They can be seen on air-planes, reading workbooks and reports and proposals, rapidly turning past all of the interesting parts of the newspaper to focus on the business news. One of them, a college president, speaking to a group of librarians, prefaced his talk by saying that he felt a little awkward being among librarians, since the only things he had time to read were the photocopied materials which came across his desk. He even seemed to be proud of that statement, and there was a ripple of chuckles across the audience, chuckles which acknowledged that many among them had that same feeling of being overwhelmed by the necessary reading their jobs required.

When I encounter people like that, I want to say, "Did you know that, when England was in its darkest days during World War II, Winston Churchill went home at night and read Jane Austen?" There is particular pleasure in that picture for me, because I remember standing in Jane Austen's home and reading the correspondence she had with the Prince Regent. In one letter, he wrote that because she had such a large audience among the people, a book about the royal family of Saxe-Coburg, perhaps a romance that would give English-men a bit of the history of that royal house, would be met with an enthusiastic response. Being a Prince Regent, he communicated through his secretary. Being Jane Austen, she replied directly and honestly, saying she was quite incapable of writing such a book. She would just have to keep up with her own kind of story. I think of that exchange of letters whenever I am in conversation with an earnest writer of children's books—and they must be among the most earnest people of our society—who says that he talks with children and asks them what they are interested in, and then goes home and writes about it. It is clear that, in many instances, this leads to a successful living for the author, and the results may even give much pleasure and information to children. *However, I do not believe that any child ever said he would be interested in a book that would tell about how a spider saves a pig's life or how two children lived for a week in the Metropolitan Museum. Competence can be prompted by the expressed needs of others; genius cannot.*

This is not to say that we do not need the works of the competent as well as of the geniuses. What we do need is access to all kinds of materials to read for different purposes, in different moods, at different times, and in different ways. It seems like a very simple idea, but, like most simple ideas, it is not easy to achieve.

Someone has said that the single idea that is most typical of our American society, and the one which has made it great, is access. Other countries may have surpassed us in the traditions of their great schools and universities, but we have made ours accessible in ways which uniquely distinguish us. Even with the constant constraints of funding and the low priority placed upon support, our libraries provide access in a distinctive way. Until the great chains of bookstores made their way into shopping malls and to downtown streets, I could not have counted them as providing great access to books for our country. That is not to disparage the "personal" bookstores—the browsers' stores many of us have loved—but they have tended always to be directed toward those of us with acquired tastes for reading who are used to searching for what we need. There is a bookstore in Chicago that I avoid at all costs. I know that it is likely to have what I want, but I would rather wait weeks to borrow the book from my local library than to venture in where the exceedingly knowledgeable proprietor would tell me exactly where on the shelves I could find the title, and then shout at me if I veered an inch off

73

course in moving toward it. Bookstores and libraries, in my view, may indeed be built along straight lines, but they should all allow for the quirkiness of their users. The mark of genius in their arrangements of materials is shown when order is happily combined with idiosyncracy.

The ideal in terms of access comes close to achievement when there are enough materials on a topic to tantalize us without overwhelming us, and when we are required to make some choices to find and use what we want and need. As I write this, I think of Francie Nolan, the heroine of Betty Smith's *A Tree Grows in Brooklyn,* conscientiously reading her way through the collection at her neighborhood public library, working alphabetically through the shelves, but treating herself occasionally by asking the librarian for a good book for a girl her age. As I recall, the librarian had two books at the desk, offered alternatively in response to Francie's request. There was some choice there, but that is not enough to satisfy most of us. We go through life expecting some books to reach out and touch us, or, when they cannot do that, we want, whether we know it or not, to have someone or something call our attention to what we should not miss.

The various views regarding individual selection of materials make up a kind of folklore among librarians, a folklore in which we recall, of course, our successes. We are usually unaware of our failures. When Frances Clarke Sayers, noted children's librarian from the New York Public Library, traveled the country some years ago, speaking to librarians and teachers about the joys of books and reading, she told a story about a little girl who came to her one day and asked for *Alice in Orchestralia.* Sayers knew the book about the child who learned all about the different instruments in the orchestra, and she plunged enthusiastically into the section of books about orchestras and musical instruments, but drew no response from her patron. Finally, the little girl said, "I'm not reading orchestras; I'm reading Alices." In its simplicity, that story has always epitomized for me the need for understanding in what is nowadays called the "reference interview." The librarian may make associations from words and requests which are highly reasonable but totally inaccurate. Children, especially, may be following selection patterns of their own, and these call for more, not less, expertise on the part of the person helping them. That little girl in New York, for example, might have found several books in the catalog in which Alice was the first word of the title, but she would have needed guidance from a well-informed children's librarian to discover other books where there was a major character named Alice. With confidence established, she might have been lured into reading about people with other names.

The hard part about encouraging independence in selection of materials to read is to know when to push, when to pull, and, perhaps most importantly, when to stop. This is really analogous to the matter of encouraging independence in the process of reading. Parents and other interested adults sometimes assume that once a child starts to read, he is on his own. In truth, he still needs encouragement and guidance. This may be easy in homes where questions like, "What does Mike Royko say about Jane Byrne today?" or "Have you finished the Michener article in *TV Guide*?" are natural parts of conversation. In homes such as these, children may easily get the idea that reading is an essential part of living, and that what one reads and what one thinks about reading are interesting subjects to talk about.

Even when literacy is not a problem, there are families who do not have the time or the know-how to integrate reading into their common lives. We can attribute these lacks to insufficient time or to the prevalence of other media, notably television, but there is more to it than that. The child who saw his mother seated with a book in her hand for the first time, and who told a neighbor she was inside watching a book, tells a good deal about television and that family's uses of time. However, as an enthusiastic television and movie fan myself, I think we create paper tigers about the encroachments of these other media. The greater issue is discipline. We are fond of quoting the biblical statement about having times to live, to die, to sow, and to reap, and successful families set times to read, to share, to view, and to talk.

We value privacy and quiet in our lives today, and it seems to me this heightened emphasis should, in the long run, be good for reading. In establishing the balance between interest and meddling, parents need to allow some privacy on the part of their children when it comes to their choices for reading. Not every book will move their intelligence quotients up a notch, and some may even seem to retard their social progress. I am thinking here of the riddle and joke books which are a temporary cult among almost all young readers, and which must be shared to be thoroughly enjoyed. But the child needs the freedom to read some books and not have to comment on them, perhaps not even to admit that he has them at home. When the interest of parents and other adults is steady, they do not have to quiz their children about each book. It is sufficient to open up discussions that allow children to talk about their reading and its major trends.

A few weeks ago, I was talking with an older woman who told me about the different ways her children had turned out. The two girls were older, and she had been very eager, very careful, with their reading. She took them to the library, chose their books (although she described it as "helping to choose") and in general guided them carefully. Her son was some years younger, and when he came along, she was more relaxed. She also felt she didn't have the time to spend with him as she had with her daughters, but she did encourage him to read. When she found what she described as "those awful books boys have to read" tucked under his mattress, she was so embarrassed she didn't know how to talk to him about them, so, after worrying about it for a while, she let it go. Now that her three children are adults, she says, they are all competent, successful people, but only her son is a really enthusiastic reader. He reads with the same exuberance with which he read as a child, while her daughters only skim newspapers or magazines and rarely touch books. Since I am a librarian, she asks me why they are so different.

Both her story and her question stimulate some thought. No two children, even in the same family, are raised in exactly the same environment. Age and sex, and the size and location of their rooms are only a few of the factors that distinguish them. Without realizing it, my acquaintance illustrates that some of us, as parents, achieve openness by default rather than by design. Lack of concern does not always result in stimulating children to read, but, without ever having met him, I picture that little boy watching his sisters read with assurance, and deciding that he would get to be as good at it as they were. Free of the help his mother lavished on them, he approached reading as his own thing to do, and thus acquired a lifelong pleasure.

There is a need for a similar balance, in the alliance between teachers and parents, which encourages reading. Laughing at the content of basal readers is about as reasonable as laughing at crutches or hearing aids. Children who are acquiring reading skills need to do so in an environment that encourages them, not just by letting them work at the tasks before them, but also by pointing to some of the values those skills will help them to achieve. Hearing someone read well at a time when one is struggling with basic skills can be as encouraging and stimulating as listening to a piano virtuoso when the scales are taxing our fingers and ears. Is it hopeless, in our time, to speak of oral reading as a possible family or school pastime? I think not. This is one area where the media have compensated elegantly for some of the shortcomings of our own backgrounds. People today have not usually had to read orally as much as earlier generations in school, and it is hardly surprising that they are not usually as good at it. But they have access to a considerable variety of recordings in which oral reading is an enjoyable art. Libraries provide these, too, and they can help children make the connection between reading as a skill and reading as an art.

I do not want to pass too quickly over the problem of adults who are reluctant to read aloud with children. Besides the very obvious fact that most of us get better at doing something as we do it more often, these adults may need to keep in mind that others seldom criticize what we do for them when the motivation is to give them pleasure. A teacher or parent may read with some self-consciousness, or with an awful accent, but the listeners enjoy the experience because it is time that is devoted to them and to reading.

Some of this same enjoyment is, I believe, what keeps some less than excellent classics alive. While there are many books that live on through the generations because of their timeless excellence—and I note the current centenaries of *Pinocchio* and *Heidi*—there are others that endure because people remember them from their childhoods and introduce them to new generations. The healthy tolerance and curiosity of children allow them to respond happily to these, even when the charm of the book or its special message may have outlived its time. Much as I enjoyed it as a child, I have to put *Black Beauty* in this category. I remember my father and mother, both of them enthusiastic horseback riders, explaining to me about bits and bridles and parts of the horse's body so that I would understand why Beauty suffered so. They enhanced my enjoyment of the book, just as the teachers who read *The Box Car Children* year after year make it popular, even while the quality of the book is questionable. For classics, too, there is a time to live and a time to die.

Librarians have grown more tolerant of some of the kinds of books that, for years, they had overlooked. A notable example of the series books that libraries for a long time prided themselves on not providing are the Nancy Drew mysteries. I remember my own startled reaction when a worldly-wise friend argued with me over dinner about the long-standing alliance he claimed must have existed between libraries and the publishers of such books. As an economist, he was sure that libraries had determined not to purchase the books and to say instead to patrons, "But you can get them for forty-nine cents at Woolworth's"—as was the case when I was a child. As a result, the publisher, selling copies by the millions rather than the thousands, was able to keep the price very low and the books very accessible. A cold chill ran through me as I thought this might indeed be true. If libraries refused to stock *Charlotte's Web* or *Winnie the Pooh* or *Tom Sawyer,* might those have become underground classics instead, selling many times the number of copies that have been sold? There is more to it than that, of course, but the conversation has haunted me as I have realized that there are significant links between publishers, booksellers, and libraries, and that ownership of books has a special significance for children who own, in their own names, very little beyond the necessities of life.

I have mixed feelings about this matter of ownership. My own misgivings are directed toward the popular program known as Reading is Fundamental. I should preface my comments by saying that, primarily because of a very committed and very persuasive friend, I contribute to Reading is Fundamental. I have visited its programs in several locations, and talked with its staff members and many of the adults who make it work. I think I understand its purposes and procedures. My contributions are rather like those of the nonbeliever who occasionally sends money to a religious group. It is just possible that these people are right, and, if they are, I want to help them. In any case, they probably do not do much damage. But, when I have stood in elementary school activity rooms and seen the array of inexpensive books spread out on tables, and the children ushered in to make their choices, I have wondered whether, if all that effort and money were directed toward the school library media program instead, we might not have the best opportunities to encourage young readers. I am aware of the argument that there is special pride in ownership, and that, especially for young children who own very little, the idea of owning a book is of great significance. I am also aware that there are special problems today in teaching what community ownership is. But my response is that it may indeed be much better to have opportunity and the ability to choose among many different books, and to exchange them freely, rather than to be limited to owning one or the few that one can acquire in several years of participation in Reading is Fundamental.

I mentioned the ability to choose among materials. This is a seldom-taught library skill which considerably enhances the pleasure and the value of reading. Picking a book for one's-self means knowing more exactly what one really wants, and being able to identify the elements of a book that will satisfy that want. It is not as simple as being directed toward the third grade table nor, for adults, to the best sellers or the mysteries. It is the ability to use the book's title, one's knowledge about the author, the statement on the jacket, the date of copyright, the index, the chapter headings, the format and the feel of the book itself, and to decide whether it will really provide us with what we want. It goes without saying that we need to know something about ourselves and the subject or information or form of satisfaction we want from the book, to integrate all of this information and to act on it. The current emphasis on orienting students to the library at all levels of education should assist in this. The most successful of these programs are really integrated, so that the student gets the idea that the goal is to be self-sufficient, not only about how to find materials in the library, but also about how to select and use them independently and creatively.

Without the ability to choose, people can't use the wealth of materials they may have available within their reach. And the biggest and best libraries, bookstores, or any other kind of collection of reading materials are without meaning, without value, if they can not be used intelligently. Unfortunately, not even all librarians are dedicated to the idea of making people self-sufficient in choosing what they want. Nor are all libraries or bookstores well-designed to encourage or even to allow for this self-sufficiency. I suppose part of this is based on the unspoken thought that we are revealing some of the mystique of librarianship if we get to the point where everyone operates well in a library without having to ask for help. And sometimes, this is because librarians overestimate the knowledge of their patrons. A friend of mine who works in a major university's research library loves her job, and because she answers the telephone when scholars call to check a reference, often feels a part of the great research which emanates from the university. There are times when she has even discovered a new resource to help them in their work. As for the university's students, she thinks they are among the brightest and the best, and, pointing to them busily searching among the ranks of card catalogs, or seated at index tables, she will proudly say, "Look at them! They really use this library!" Indeed they do, and they have worked out, among themselves, a buddy system to get the help they need, because they have learned it does not work to ask my friend or her library colleagues for it.

Why do I reveal what is to me an embarrassing shortcoming in a librarian's attitude? Only to make the point that real access to materials involves service, and service, in turn, involves attitudes as well as knowledge. As more and more people catch on to the fascination of some library tools, notably computers, there is, I think, real danger that we may forget or even thwart their purposes which are, almost always, to lead us on to something else. Having a pile of references laid out on large sheets of paper is not an improvement over handwriting on papyrus unless it allows us more time for the thought that goes with our reading of the references themselves. But to many people, these computer searches have become so valuable in themselves that they do not even check the quality of the references, much less the specific content of the material. "Look at how much there is!" has become a familiar cry, but it scarcely matches the more appropriate one for a searcher for information: "This is what I've learned!"

I am dwelling too much on skills, perhaps, and I surprise myself by doing so, because I do not think too much about skills at all. Perhaps that proves their value best: when mastered, we can take them for granted. But among those skills, I must include critical reading. The enthusiasts for reading whom I mentioned earlier sometimes leave us with the impression that all reading is good. It may be, but not everything we read is accurate, nor can we accept it all passively. This is so readily understood by a sophisticated audience that I should, perhaps, not even mention it, but it is a part of the link between reading and successful living. Knowing how to check for facts and to compare ideas or perspectives, noting the dates that may explain discrepancies in various reports, and even developing the habit of taking notes with care and double-checking on their accuracy before using them are all a part of critical reading. In this area, as in the instilling of the value of reading for its own sake, observers who benefit from the careful reading of others probably learn as much about the need for critical reading as they need to develop it as a habit for themselves.

The biggest stumbling-block to any effort to build interest in reading as an activity shared by families is illiteracy. The fact that there continues to be a stubborn percentage of adults who are not able to read is frustrating because it limits many kinds of communications among schools, libraries, and the adult community. Perhaps we need to be less subtle about the fact in our work with children. While it is certainly difficult to make dedicated, competent readers of children who are struggling for even more basic needs in life, and while illiteracy is always closely tied to poverty, it may be that we do not urge the children, as they experience early successes with reading, to share those successes with their parents. Adults who are literate seem always to be embarrassed that others are not. Jonathan Kozol has recommended a kind of national crusade in which literacy would spread almost by sheer force of numbers and moral commitment, with adults teaching other adults in individual settings. But if it has been proved effective that reading parents make their children want to read because they want to be like them, it seems possible to me that children learning to be literate should have some of that same positive effect on their illiterate parents.

I remember, as a child, watching several scenes that were played out in the classroom of the urban parochial school I attended. One of my classmates, Clara, was a perennial truant and, by fifth-grade, was well on her way to fulfilling her mother's vociferous descriptions of her as a tramp. Whenever her Italian-speaking mother brought her back to school, or came to talk to Sister about her, she did so, dramatically and in Italian, at the front of the room, often holding Clara by the ear and waving to the rest of the class to witness her problems with this girl. I was always frightened but fascinated. I pictured that something like that could happen to me if I one day stayed home sick and my mother decided to question how sick I was and to humiliate me in front of Sister and the rest of the class, but I knew it could not be as exciting, with my mother speaking plain English, even if she used her maddest tone of voice. What I realize now was that to Clara, it must have seemed as if all of us—Sister, her mother, and the rest of the class—were her opposition. Those confrontations come to mind because thinking about reading and successful living makes me think of the importance of strong bonds between many parts of our education system, but it is important that those bonds create cooperation rather than confrontation, and that they do not form alliances among some groups to the detriment of others. Our history suggests that too often, that is the way it has been.

Another incident with a child who never succeeded at school comes to my mind. Some thirty years ago, when I worked in the children's room of a branch library, I had gotten to know a boy who was too old and too big for the elementary class with whom he used to visit the library. The biggest challenge he presented was trying to find books for him that were exactly 150 pages in length. His teacher would accept no less for his book reports, and he would accept no more, since that was what was required. The day came when Vernon was needed in his father's shop, and he had reached the age when he was no longer required to go to school. His first stop was the library, and he was ready then to turn in his current 150-pages book and his library card. I pushed the card back across the desk. "Here, you'll want this," I said. He looked surprised. "But doesn't it all go together?" he asked. We had convinced Vernon that libraries and books were a part of education, but we had not made him aware that they are a part of life beyond school. I doubt that our brief conversation persuaded him entirely, but he did walk out with his library card tucked in his shirt pocket where it could be seen as some continuing identity for him, and he also walked out with a book—less than 150 pages long. Perhaps because he did not leave school in some formal commencement ceremony where no one would have mentioned that public libraries were still available to him, he got the message directly: reading and libraries and schools and life are linked, yes, but there is even more to all of it than that.

As a librarian, I may have been expected to write about

specific materials or lists which help to make the connection between reading and successful living. There are plenty of both—books and lists. The titles change and the changes are often for the better. We certainly have a greater number of appealing books for reluctant readers than we had when I started my career as a children's librarian, and, for the most part, we know more about the causes of poor reading and the tragedies of unemployment and unhappiness that it can cause. That does not always seem to have increased our understanding of the individual reader, but, in the long run, it comes back to that. *People become readers one by one. They make their commitments to reading on an individual basis.* They choose their books according to their individual needs and tastes. Occasionally, they may be turned off by an individual title, or simply uninterested in it. They will pick up the free lists that are laid out invitingly for them, but they may find those lists as frustrating as they are stimulating. The most intriguing titles seem never to be available, and some of the second or third choices may be disappointments. And yet if, somewhere along the line, reading has proved to be a pleasure and a help in life, people do not give up on it. In the long run, reading is the ally for each one of us, and the alliances we may form to encourage it are a very important part of the story of reading and successful living.

RESPONSES AND DISCUSSION

Peggy Sullivan introduced the discussion session for her paper by reminding us that siblings in the family are often vital to the reading and success relationship. In our highly mobile society, with so many mothers working, siblings may well be the ones to make the greatest difference in how children develop both stability and communication skills. The tenuous relationships among individuals and generations, particularly in the single-parent families, tend to strengthen the relationships among siblings. Today, many fourth graders are the role models for younger brothers and sisters.

M. RICHARD ROBINSON, *President and Chief Executive Officer, Scholastic Magazines, Inc.*

Marian Brown and Nancy Larrick have both mentioned the importance of preschool beginnings of reading, but I must tell you that the number of books children are exposed to before they get to school is relatively small. The support system just isn't there—the teacher, the school—and there is little built-in motivation. This is something we definitely should do something about. The teacher is a catalyst for book reading, and the teacher-parent-child triangle should begin earlier. It is unrealistic to think that most parents of children either at the preschool level or older, are going to be able to organize themselves to get quality literature without help from someone. Nothing happens without access to books, and early book ownership has a great effect on later reading. The critical years during which parents, children, and teachers should be working together to lay the groundwork for lifetime reading occur when children are between four and eight years of age.

The recent growth of private schools, funded by parents, suggests the importance to the public schools of getting parents involved—the people with a personal stake in the school, the 20 to 30 percent of households with children in school. If they are not involved, they may leave the public school system, thereby further polarizing our society. Parents, teachers, and children are being brought together in part by their growing realization of their minority position in society. If the school creates practical vehicles for participation and partnership to happen, it will happen. We know this from our own business: one of every two teachers in elementary school uses paperback book clubs for children to buy inexpensive books, and some twelve to fourteen million children participate in buying books from clubs. Some 200,000,000 books reach children through books clubs such as ours every year.

There are many examples of successful parent/school/child interaction with reading opportunity as the goal:

In Houston, Operation Fail Safe involves parents in setting goals for their children's progress in basic skills, and provides a monitoring process;

Oakland developed a sustained silent reading and paperback saturation project which parents help administer and monitor in the middle and junior high schools;

In Knoxville, whole communities participate in celebrating RIF distribution days—which are really family celebrations—of reading and books.

Many other examples could be cited. We know that the principal is probably the key person in assuming leadership for providing parents with ways to be involved in their children's reading and learning, and, where programs have been successful, principals have usually been the motivators.

As we go through a period of prolonged economic stress— for families as well as for institutions—we must learn to make more productive use of the talents of organizations like PTA and National School Volunteers, as well as individuals—parents and otherwise. People in the community need to be asked to contribute skills and resources in science, technology, and business, which the schools cannot otherwise provide. At the extreme, industry may need to fund some portions of the school program directly, as in Pittsburgh, where U.S. Steel has "adopted" several high schools in order to insure that the company will get the technical skills it needs in the future. There are pitfalls, if carried too far, but all community resources need to be carefully considered and blended into a support patterns appropriate to the times.

We all know, and many of the speakers have said, that teachers are under great pressure to teach basic skills, but the community, and parents in particular, must be made aware that reading for pleasure is the road to higher literacy and higher learning. Schools and public librarians can be of tremendous help in fostering this concept, and in encouraging parents to read at home with children. Freedom to choose the book one wants to read from among exciting alternatives is a powerful motivation to read, but so too is book ownership itself. We found in studies that children who owned some books of their own finished reading them a higher percentage of the time than those they chose (just as freely) from the library. There is also the joy of re-reading a book of one's own.

The importance of access cannot be overstated. We are used to access to the things we want or might want: it is one of the hallmarks of our society, and one of the things that has made it great. The schools have the responsibility to see to it that books are widely available in the school and in the community, in libraries to borrow, and through clubs, fairs, RIF programs, and the like, to own and keep and make a part of oneself. It is especially important that as the microcomputer and other communication and learning tools receive more widespread use in middle-class homes, we ensure that both books and these other learning tools are available to poor children as well.

An important barrier to access is censorship, the reverse of free access. We can see an increase in censorship efforts from both the Right and the Left. Members of the family-school partnership must stand firm for the right of parents to provide guidance for what their own children shall read (or what television programs they shall watch), while at the same time not be permitted to interfere with the rights of other parents and children to make their own decisions in these matters.

I see the future of the microcomputer and videodiscs as having enormously positive potential effects on education and on literacy. The informational book may be replaced by information stored on a computer, but children's literature should emerge stronger than ever. The new cable and video technologies will provide a great variety of experiences to children, and they are well-suited to book-related programming.

In summary, I would like to see a formal program in every school and school district, sponsored by school administrators and supported by the boards of education and the community, which involves parents and other family members, in a structured way, in the aid and reinforcement of children's reading.

JACK CASSIDY, *Professor of Reading, Millersville State College, Pennsylvania, and president-elect, International Reading Association*

One of the most important things that a parent can do—especially a male parent—is to read himself and let the child witness his enjoyment. Sex differences affect reading tremendously. Boys exceed girls in remedial reading rooms by a ratio of anywhere from four-to-one to forty-to-one. In the elementary schools, girls score better than boys on practically every standardized achievement test. Girls use libraries more, too, as do adult women. Boys receive more negative feedback about their reading than girls do; girls are praised more often in class for reading well. Boys do not perceive reading as a masculine activity. When shown a group of objects in behavioral tests, a group of objects which included a book, children identified the book as an appropriate gift for a girl. This was true in the United States and Canada, but not in other countries.

This image of reading as a feminine activity, although doubtless reinforced in schools, begins in the homes, where it is implicitly and explicitly expressed that if you are a boy, there is something wrong with you if you want to read a book. I agree with others who have said that training to be a reader must start in early childhood and that it must start with the parents and the home. We need more parent training, and more of such things as workshops for adults on critical thinking and the links between thinking, reading, and successful living. The work of the family-school partnership should not be too narrow in scope, but it must be planned and phased so that schools and communities can tackle whatever part of it they are ready for and able to effect at a particular time.

Summary
Lester Asheim

(William Rand Kenan Jr. Professor of Library Science, The University of North Carolina at Chapel Hill.)

My assignment in this program is to move us toward a Tentative Agenda of Recommendations—not by introducing recommendations of my own, but rather by recapping for your attention, the major recommendations that have surfaced in the papers and the discussions in this richly-packed day and one-half. Any such summary inevitably introduces the bias of the person who does the abstracting, of course, and I am afraid that, with a captive audience and a lectern in front of me, I may not be able to control an occasional comment of my own. I presume I do not have to tell you to listen to what I say about what I think *you* said with a pinch of corrective salt ever ready at hand.

Although we touched upon many other social and educational matters in the course of our discussions, I shall try to focus on those statements and comments which seem to me to carry recommendations, overt or implicit, which could help us, the participant organizations, and their individual members, to begin a program of implementation of stronger *family*-school partnership—in the sense that Nancy Larrick and Peggy Sullivan urged it, with the emphasis on the total family, not just the parents—in the promotion of reading. In this context, here are some of the points that most impressed me as useful signposts on our road toward a program of action.

Dr. Palmer's suggestion, supported by Mrs. Thomas, that we must be clear about what it is we are seeking to accomplish is certainly, in my view, a proper place to begin. The title of our symposium, "Reading and Successful Living," is a provocative title, but it is so open-ended that we might all go off in entirely different and even conflicting directions, and still feel we are faithfully adhering to the name of the game. During this meeting a number of different criteria were mentioned related to what reading contributes to "successful living," from appreciation of beauty that is in itself satisfying, and the sheer joy of reading, to preparation for a specific job and then growing in the job; from a better understanding of the self to understanding others; from increased income to increased knowledge; from the pleasure of intellectual challenge to the basic ability to read the instructions on a package. Whichever of those we mean to encompass, or if we really mean to include them all, we should be clear and in agreement about from the beginning. As Palmer reminds us, "Even if the goals seem clear by implication, it can be useful to state them." I would alter "can be useful" to "is absolutely essential."

Several of you have referred to the specific suggestions contained in the paper of Duncan and Palmer. I will not repeat all of those items here; let me rather suggest that as you begin the planning of programs or the search for suggestions for program possibilities, you refer to these papers for ideas.

I liked Fay's recommendation, seconded by Leveridge and others, that our focus should be, not primarily on the *basic* skills or minimum essentials, but rather on the higher levels of performance. I am quite willing to accept his evidence, and the evidence of my own experience with the students who have come out of the schools to the university, that the current programs do know how to teach the basic skills, and have demonstrated that populations that traditionally have difficulty with reading can learn to do so and gain benefits from programs directed to their specific problems. The real failure has been the inability—or unwillingness—of many who have the basic skills to undertake the higher-level applications of those skills with materials that challenge and stimulate and enrich. If we are to develop a program looking toward constructive change, it should be a program that will build upon and go beyond the basics.

While Palmer urges us to be more aware of the resources and the resourcefulness of parents as partners in our work with the reading of children, he also urges us to look realistically at some of the difficulties. Many of you recognized that not all parents will be interested; not all parents will have the qualifications, nor will all parents (or teachers, for that matter) be "willing to relinquish convenience for the sake of effectiveness." But his is a call to be realistic, not discouraged, and I was particularly interested in Palmer's suggestion that there are people who can help reach children whose own parents cannot reach them, and that this could represent a potential source of support which is sometimes overlooked. Let me say that I do want to return to this theme in a moment in a darker mood, but, in the meantime, it should be noted that the positive aspect of tapping the talents of those who have a way with children was also urged by Andringa, who would have us seek persons other than parents as well. The idea of such an extensive pool of talent is attractive, but I do have serious reservations about his apparent belief that training in teaching skills, knowledge of the learning process, and the ability to teach as well as to have empathy with children are not only unnecessary but may even be a liability. This is a disturbing echo, to me as a librarian, of the once widely-held belief that all you need to be a librarian is "to just love" books. Am I being hyper-sensitive?

An important point is the one made by Palmer that many parents would be willing and eager to cooperate and contribute if they were adequately informed about the ways, the means, and the objectives of doing so. This is a challenge to both teachers and librarians to prepare materials, gather data, identify model programs, and—most especially—to disseminate them widely and wisely in ways which will attract and persuade. Many others urged a wider use of effective public relations and marketing techniques. Here, Palmer also gives us some sound guidance: we will have to make people see clearly how a working partnership can produce outcomes of the sort they themselves are seeking. This is a slight paraphrase from Palmer, who was speaking about the need to convince *teachers* that they should seek parental cooperation, but it works the other way as well; parents too must see *their* aims fostered by the relationship. But when Duncan says that "the perception of personal gain is fundamental in the motivational process," we may get a small premonition that the statement is not only a two-way street, but perhaps a double-edged sword. However, I do think it carries a positive implication, and has a far larger application, than the rather negative "what's-in-it-for-me?" attitude which it seems to suggest. At the moment, I would like it to stand, without moral or ethical overtones, as simply a basic principle of effective communication which we must bear in mind.

The call for a leavening of realism to temper our enthusiasm for a cause so patently worthwhile should also be heeded.

Fay urges us to be realistic in our expectations about the capacity of all *children* to reach certain high-level goals we are predisposed to set; Palmer reminds us that we need to set more realistic expectations about what the *parents* (and teachers) can, or would be willing, to do. Certainly it must be admitted that there are teachers who will never be satisfied with—as Fay puts it—less than a Ph.D. for everyone; certainly it is true that some parents don't see the value of schooling at all if it gives their children "ideas". In both cases, the hidden, underlying recommendation for your agenda is that we must recognize what Fay stated so forcibly: there is a vast range of talents and interests in our society at all levels; indeed, this diversity is one of the characteristics that several of the speakers urged the schools and the libraries in a democracy to preserve. As Sullivan put it, "What we need is access to all kinds of materials to read for different purposes, in different moods, at different times, and in different ways." Expectations, of what the children will be able to do and what the parents will be able to do, must be individualized. "People become readers," Sullivan reminds us, "one by one." This may be the one response in our meeting to the very essential questions raised by Fitzgerald concerning the absence, from this symposium group, of a representative of the negative or even dubious viewpoint. We did at least recognize the existence of other viewpoints and needs, despite the homogeneous membership in the symposium.

It is only natural, in a symposium whose title begins with the word, "Reading," and which is sponsored and hosted by the Center for the Book, that the major emphasis in the papers has been upon books and reading. Nevertheless, I was glad to see the broader concept of "literacy" recognized by Fay. The values which were once available almost exclusively through "reading" are now also supported by other formats. Other sources can also make a contribution to the students' ability to think, to reason, to gain information, to marshall facts, to conjure up the past, examine the present, and think to the future—"the whole new way of learning in our society"—to which Andringa referred. This is not to say that reading is identical to any of the other communication abilities: it *is* different, and it has certain strengths that none of the others possess for sharpening and demanding the exercise of the kind of critical thinking that our complex world requires. If, today, to be educated no longer means simply that one must be well-read, that is not to say that to be educated no longer requires that one be well-read. It does require that, and maybe it even requires it first, but it also requires related and new skills, and we will harm our own cause if we permit our devotion to the many-faceted meanings of "reading" to convey to others something narrow and constricting, rather than wide-reaching and liberating.

I was particularly glad to hear the admonition of many of you that we should not fear the new technology, but rather learn to use it to support and foster those values which reading has so long advanced. Time that is released by the machine's assumption of routine and repetitive duties can, as Fay suggested, be used to free the teacher and librarian to give more personalized attention to the individual student. It is not at all an impossible dream that we could learn to take the tool that has seemed to threaten the book and use it instead to promote the book. Several of you cited other specific examples of how book-promotion may be achieved. This is, as you know, precisely the point of the Center for the Book's project, and "Read More About It" feature, which appears at the end of some major prime-time television specials to recommend further reading on the subject of the program. It is time to call off the feud between book and non-book and begin to make more imaginative use of the machine in its various forms as tools to serve our purpose. As Humpty Dumpty told Alice, "The question is, which is to be master, that's all."

All of which leads me, as I warned you I might, to depart from my role of strict reporter and to speak now, out of my own prejudices, about what I consider to be perhaps the biggest challenge that faces us. I return, with a slightly different slant, to Fay's recommendation that "the school's problems with reading are not with minimums but rather with higher levels of performance." Our real task, I believe, is to build upon the teaching of reading *as such,* and to find a way to instill a recognition of the enormous value of the continuing and deepening *use* of that skill. The trouble with the popular interpretation of "back-to-basics" is that it fixes upon minimal skills rather than on deeper essentials. Once, presumably, what was "basic" about reading would have been the broadening, enlightening, enriching, and challenging nature of the intangibles in the reading experience, rather than the simple recognition of isolated groupings of letters to make isolated unrelated words. I think that is what Marilyn Miller was talking about in asking for a broader context for the term "literacy" than simply the recognition of black marks on white paper.

We may have been mistaken in accepting the thesis that the way to make reading a value in people's lives is to make it easy. If avoidance of effort were always the decisive variable, there would be no dieters, no joggers, no gardeners, no Sunday painters, nor any amateurs in any of the activities that require a developed skill or discipline. It is my belief that our reading instruction has succeeded in reducing the effort of reading for a larger segment of the population than has ever been true before; where we have failed is in the area of motivation. (Motivation in the sense Palmer suggested, i.e., "providing a channel through which the natural tendency of the flow can be facilitated"; this same idea was expressed in terms of "awareness" by Mrs. Thomas). We have failed, too, in identifying the *rewards* of reading in such a way that more than a favored few will recognize them.

But it is here, in the realm of values and in the agreement on what constitutes the "rewards"—of reading, of education, of access to ideas—that our greatest stumbling block lies. *Where "Successful Living" is identified as strict obedience to received wisdom as defined by one source and one interpreter, wide reading, diversity of viewpoints, challenges to accepted ideas, and broader understanding of other people's opinions are seen, not as values, but as dangers.*

Look at some of the values that have been stressed in our discussions today: "helping children to explore different worlds and values . . ."; "to be exposed to and try to understand the life styles of different people . . ."; "to appreciate the wonders and instruments of the man-made world . . ."; "to use books to trigger discussion when sensitive subjects involving fears or apprehensions arise . . ."; "letting children have and trust their own feelings about a book . . ."; ". . . the ability to choose . . ."; "letting a child read from a book far above that child's head when that is what the child wants . . ."; "to tolerate, indeed, cherish, difference rather than conformity . . ."; "to use books independently and freely."

I submit that every one of those goals, which I presume this group would support as desirable, are seen by many parents, not as values to which they subscribe, but as a direct attack upon the values they hold.

93

They have been used, not in defense of books and libraries, but as the reason for banning textbooks, condemning course content, and removing books from the libraries' shelves. While Palmer and Duncan make clear that there are some parents we may never be able to reach, or, upon reaching, enlist in a partnership, there is another group of parents which troubles me even more: not those who are indifferent about their children's education or, as Cody and Sullivan suggested, those too preoccupied with other burdens; but rather those who are all too willing to accept our invitation to take an active role in directing and controlling their children's reading, and that of other people's children, and that of everyone else's, child or adult. I agree with Duncan's conclusion that "perhaps our education system would better educate children if we spent more time educating parents." The problems of accomplishing this are many and varied, ranging from the hostile parent, identified by Leveridge, to the problem at quite the other end of the spectrum, identified by Rollock, of the parent who wants and needs what reading has to offer, but cannot, for a variety of social, economic, and educational reasons, be reached by the usual means of communication.

What I am suggesting is that we cannot assume that our views, simply by their self-evident rightness, will convince those who do not now share them. One of the difficulties is that one of the best convincers is the ability to read at the highest level. As Palmer suggested, those who have that, by and large, do not need convincing. Those who do not have it are deprived of the very instrument that would make those values most clear.

My point is simply to remind you that opposition does exist; that these opposing views seem absolutely right to those who hold them; and that this represents a far greater challenge than does parental indifference. There may be, therefore, hidden time bombs in some of our proposals. I said I would return to the suggestion that we find people who can reach children whose own parents cannot reach them; the darker underside of this is that often these influential persons are the opponents of free and wide reading, not the defenders of it. When we recommend that parents read the books their children are reading, we should recognize that that is precisely what the Gablers, in their Texas kitchen, and others who share their views, are recommending. When Duncan urges that we should establish the role of the parent as teacher, and that education is the responsibility of the society (and most especially the parents), he puts a strong weapon in the hands of those who would dictate a curriculum geared to their private prejudices.

Knowing all that need not discourage us if we have the conviction and the commitment that all of our speakers have urged is essential. We cannot convince others if we are not, ourselves, convinced. Our greatest vulnerability may be, as Yeats foresaw more than half a century ago: "The best lack all conviction, while the worst are full of passionate intensity."

It was the hope of the planners of this symposium, I think, that the exchange of ideas among these several groups who do share that passionate intensity about reading could lead to action designed to protect, foster, and increase a sense of the value of wide and challenging reading. Admittedly, the task is a staggering one, and in almost every aspect of American life there are indicators as Andringa pointed out, that it may be more difficult at the present time than usual. But surely our chances are better if we can reduce contention and increase cooperation, despite some polar differences in the ends people hold for education, reading, and use of social communication in all of its forms, including the book. As Duncan put it, "If communication can take place, perceptions [can] change."

Both Duncan and Andringa identified the key justification—and challenge—for the recommendations growing out of these meetings: "Both parents and educators must remember, the school belongs *to the public*." To reiterate, the school belongs to the whole public, not just to parents or teachers or librarians. The task we are being asked to undertake is not the protection of our private turfs, but the selfless promotion of an essential tool in the enhancement of the skills of critical thinking, problem-solving, the power to reason, and making of value judgments. As we look towards the future, the beneficiaries will be, not just the educators and the librarians, but the whole society, including the parents, both those who make common cause with us and those who do not comprehend or approve our purpose. Above all, the children, who will be the parents, the teachers, the movers and shakers of tomorrow, will be the beneficiaries.

PART II
Steps Toward
Forging the Partnership

The following principles and recommendations are those evolved by participants in the symposium on "Reading and Successful Living: The Family-School Partnership." The ideas and convictions are theirs; the editors have exercised the privilege of organizing them, providing details of structure and action, and in some cases, combining and/or extrapolating from one to another. Recommendations for action addressed to the local community and state levels are numbered consecutively from 1–72, and grouped under the principles to which they most closely relate; recommendations for national action, nine in number, are given separately at the end of these.

The assumption of a positive attitude is the first step in approaching the development of the working family-school partnership. It must be in place before any other steps are taken if the efforts that follow are to be productive. We commend to your attention, in this regard, the advice from Dr. Palmer's paper:

> To attempt to reach reluctant parents can be viewed as giving them more than they deserve, an uphill battle, a losing cause, or as an activity outside one's training and job description, and therefore outside one's purview; or else it can be viewed as a problem we've all lived with for too long and to which we need some answers. It can be viewed as an occasion for overcoming indifference transmitted down through generations, a constructive response to the stresses of contemporary family life, or an obligation to give every child a vision of the successful life, and the wherewithal through books to broaden and pursue that vision.
>
> Participants in this partnership who think in terms of sitting on the same side of the problem facing it side by side will make a qualitatively different contribution than those who conceive of themselves as sitting at

loggerheads. Those who think of linking up forces which are already moving or are inclined to move in the same direction, will have more success than those who don't. Those who think in terms of providing an occasion for people to choose so they can be given what they themselves say they want will be more effective promoters than those who only come full of advice. Those who come prepared to deal with categories of children will be less effective than those prepared to achieve something appropriate for each child, without regard for such labels as rich/poor (the rich child may be book-poor), gifted/learning disabled, good reader/poor reader. Those prepared to let a child read or be read to from a book far above that child's head when that is what the child wants will be more successful than one whose otherwise valid ideas about the developmental suitability of different books are applied in ways that are rigid and inflexible. The teacher or librarian who is willing to collaborate with parents by correspondance and not exclusively face to face will achieve a wider outreach—and in the process eventually will achieve more face to face interaction. The teacher prepared to deal with individual differences in parents, just as must be done with children, will enjoy the process more and and be more effective. The school staffer who is prepared to take advantage of the specialized skills and resources parents can bring to the partnership will be more successful than one who tries to do the whole job alone. The participant who is prepared for the value and forms of participation to evolve from the process of participation itself will experience more of the gratification of creating than will one who wants everything spelled out in advance by someone else. All these preconceptions will need to be considered in designing the symbols and images of the partnership, and in framing descriptions of roles, goals, and processes.

John W. Gardner, one of America's most creative thinkers about both education and community involvement, had this to say in his book, *Excellence:*

An important thing to understand about any institution or social system is that it doesn't move unless it is pushed. And what is generally needed is not a mild push but a solid jolt. If the push is not administered by vigorous and purposeful leaders, it will be administered eventually by an aroused citizenry or by a crisis.

Mr. Gardner also urged, more than a decade and a half ago, the importance of "raising reading on the national agenda."

It often takes just one determined person, armed with energy, conviction, a good sense of timing and the gift of persuasion, to begin the process of moving the social system or any part of it toward desirable change. Some individual must fire up a group to take the initiative relative to each of the following recommendations, but it won't be the same group in every situation. We have just indicated some possibilities for making a start, but there are certainly others, whether we have thought to mention them or not.

It is not expected that any one community, school district, library, organization, or home can carry out all of the ideas and projects proposed. We have offered a multitude of choices, because we believed that would be most helpful to you. Please bear this in mind so that you won't feel overwhelmed by all the ideas that follow. Realize as well that if every school district or community took action on just one recommendation and carried it through productively, the cumulative effect countrywide would be tremendous!

We urge you to go ahead and do whatever and as much as you can with the suggestions we have made. Adapt and combine them, in whatever way will best help to develop, in your own situation, a family-school partnership capable of incorporating reading into a more successful and satisfying life for every child.

Principles

I. READING IS CRUCIAL TO SUCCESSFUL LIVING IN OUR SOCIETY HOWEVER SUCCESS IS DEFINED.

II. ACCESS OF MANY KINDS IS ESSENTIAL TO ATTAINING THE READING EXPERIENCE AND TO BECOMING AND IDENTIFYING ONESELF AS A READER.

III. THE SOCIETY HAS A STAKE IN IMPROVING THE READING ABILITY OF ALL ITS CITIZENS. LITERACY DEVELOPMENT AND THE PROGRAMS THAT MAKE IT POSSIBLE MUST CONTINUE TO BE TREATED AS NATIONAL PRIORITY ISSUES, HOWEVER OR FROM WHATEVER LEVEL OF GOVERNMENT THEY MAY BE FUNDED.

IV. ADEQUATE FISCAL SUPPORT FOR TRAINED PROFESSIONAL STAFF AND MATERIALS TO OPERATE READING AND LIBRARY PROGRAMS IS ESSENTIAL.

V. AN ONGOING PROGRAM OF FAMILY-SCHOOL PARTNERSHIP DEPENDS UPON HIGH-LEVEL POLICY COMMITMENT ON THE PART OF THE SCHOOL SYSTEM.

VI. A STRONG FAMILY-SCHOOL PARTNERSHIP FOUNDED UPON MUTUAL TRUST AND RESPECT IS AT THE HEART OF COMMUNITY PARTICIPATION IN AND SUPPORT FOR READING AND LIBRARY DEVELOPMENT PROGRAMS.

VII. MAXIMUM PARTICIPATION OF THE WIDEST POSSIBLE RANGE OF PERSONS AND AGENCIES IS A FUNDAMENTAL NECESSITY TO THE DEVELOPMENT OF A READING COMMUNITY.

VIII. EARLY CHILDHOOD PRESCHOOL EXPERIENCES WITHIN THE FAMILY UNIT, AND AS PART OF DAYCARE AND OTHER LEARNING/PLAY GROUPS, CAN PROVIDE THE STRONGEST POSSIBLE BASE FOR LATER READING DEVELOPMENT.

IX. PRESERVICE AND CONTINUING EDUCATION FOR TEACHERS, LIBRARIANS, AND ADMINISTRATORS MUST BE PROVIDED ON A GREATLY EXPANDED SCALE IF FULLY EFFECTIVE READING DEVELOPMENT PROGRAMS ARE TO BECOME A REALITY FOR ALL CHILDREN.

X. LEARNING APPLICATIONS OF VIDEO AND COMPUTERS SHOULD BE THOROUGHLY EXPLORED AND ACCEPTED FOR USE IN THE READING DEVELOPMENT PROGRAM AS POWERFUL TOOLS IN THE HANDS OF TEACHERS AND STUDENTS, BUT TECHNOLOGY, WITH ITS MANY BY-PRODUCTS WHICH MUST BE *READ*, CANNOT BE EXPECTED TO REPLACE READING.

Principles and Recommendations for Action

STATE AND LOCAL
(Classroom, Library, School Building and District, Home, Community, and State)

I. READING IS CRUCIAL TO SUCCESSFUL LIVING IN OUR SOCIETY, HOWEVER SUCCESS IS DEFINED.

An expectation of basic functional literacy, a necessity for coping/survival at even a minimum level, is a reasonable goal for virtually all United States citizens. The nation has largely met this goal for the vast majority; the remaining barrier to the achievement of total basic literacy relates primarily to older citizens—many of them foreign born—and to young people who have dropped out of high school. Important social, political, and economic, as well as educational, issues are related to the school—and in effect, the reading—drop-out problem.

Full command of high-level reading competence, at a level that permits a significant social contribution and influence, enables individuals to recognize, reorder, synthesize, and extrapolate meaning to which their experience has already provided an introduction. We have called this high level of competence *influential literacy.* A greater degree of self-determination, respect, responsibility, confidence, fulfillment and aesthetic enjoyment of life, as well as comfortable adjustment to change, are among the benefits that the higher levels of reading competence can bestow. The skills honed by such levels of literacy are in fact the very skills utilized in absorbing and processing information from *all* sources, and which make possible inferential thinking, problem solving, and other managerial and entrepreneurial abilities.

In short, the nation's and the schools' chief challenges vis-a-vis reading are no longer related so much to basic minimums, as with achievement of higher levels of performance. We have demonstrated that we *do* know how to teach the mechanics of reading successfully; indeed, the present emphasis on basic processes, and on minimums, may be a negative force working

104

against the need for students to apply skills in increasingly demanding situations, in such a way that content and meaning is understood and assimilated. *The need for developing these high levels of reading competency is the most critical need in American reading instruction.* The definition of functional literacy must be constantly upgraded to keep pace with the literacy demands of ever more complex jobs. According to a recent study, the average difficulty level of work materials is at tenth to twelfth-grade reading level, and some 98 percent of jobs surveyed have some literacy requirement (see references at the end of Fay paper).

RECOMMENDATIONS

1. *Undertake a multi-level awareness campaign*—at the national, state, and community levels, to inform the public and to promote recognition of the distinction between minimal literacy and the level of literacy required for successful living in today's world. Special efforts must be made to bring this awareness to the attention of all legislative and governing bodies: the Congress, state, municipal and county officials, and legislators. This is necessary to give balance to the representations by some groups who claim the need, for all students, is solely for more emphasis on basic mechanical reading skills.

ACTION: Working through their local, state and national units, the four national professional associations whose concerns initiated these recommendations should galvanize this campaign, with coordinating support from the Center for the Book, involving business, civic and trade associations, and the communications industry. Successful living in our society, what constitutes success in various life roles for different people, what it takes to achieve it, and how reading plays a role, should be talked about, written about, illustrated in classrooms, club meetings, newspapers, radio, television talk shows, and the like.

2. *Feature/publicize people*, nationally and locally, to whom a book has made a great difference in transforming or enhancing life, and encourage discussion and publicity about the books that meant a great deal to them for one reason or another. (See Suggested Readings for *Books That Made the Difference* by Sabine, for follow up.) Feature and publicize local families in which reading is regularly a shared activity, highlighting interests,

hobbies, and areas of expertise, in order to bring home the immediate relevance to them of reading. Achievement and enjoyment of life, work, and leisure by individuals should be linked to their reading habits.

ACTION: PTAs and public libraries can spearhead a community hunt for families and individuals to publicize in the newspaper, in exhibits, on bulletin boards, and over radio and television. They should enlist service clubs in their search, as well as public relations departments of local industries, encouraging those in charge to highlight the reading habits of their most productive workers and their families.

3. *Action research or fact-finding* should be undertaken locally to identify aspects of home-family and community environment (agencies, programs or persons), that presently foster reading for enjoyment and self-enhancement, and conversely, factors that seem to militate against this kind of reading. Once in possession of these facts, a program of reinforcement could be drawn up, or corrective steps identified, and plans made to improve the reading environment.

ACTION: local IRA and PTA units should collaborate on this project with the advice and cooperation of the district school administrator, the director of the public library and/or trustees, and the school library media specialists. Members of Friends of Libraries groups can be especially helpful with this undertaking.

4. *A community-wide campaign* of forums, meetings, and interviews could be launched for perhaps an intensive month-long emphasis on *goals* and *futures*—for the individual, the family, and for the community. Questions might include: "What would I like to do by 1990? What do I want to be by 1990? What would I like to have for my family by 1990? What would I like to have happen in my community by 1990? In my schools by 1990? The role of reading and of libraries would be outlined in relation to all goals and dreams. Special focus would be on career possibilities—career choices for young people; second career choices for older people. The result would be to help people to think, help children to learn about the role of work in one's life, explore personal qualities; and begin to prepare and be deliberate in making choices, career and otherwise. One or more special presentations might be featured for goals presented in written or graphic form, with prizes given to the most original and those that make the best use of resource materials.

ACTION: This community campaign could be sponsored and supported by the schools, in conjunction with local business and industry, and business men's and women's organizations. There would be an opportunity here to promote new kinds of careers for women, and acclimate people to the idea of second career contributions from older people.

5. *Information should be made widely available* to parents and to other adults who work with youth as counselors, advocates, ministers, or supervisors, about books which might help to reinforce discussions of or solutions for life crisis situations such as parental divorce, death, teen pregnancy, addiction, and depression.

ACTION: The school library media specialists should initiate this project, in collaboration with school psychologists, public library staffs, ministerial alliances, and family service and other youth agencies and organizations.

II. ACCESS OF MANY KINDS IS ESSENTIAL TO ATTAINING THE READING EXPERIENCE AND TO BECOMING AND IDENTIFYING ONESELF AS A READER.

Physical access to books is the kind of access that the word brings most readily to mind. Obviously, one cannot read if there is nothing at hand to read. Nor can one read if the tools to crack the symbolic code and get at the ideas, ie., mechanical decoding skills are lacking. But beyond this, "access" carries broader implications than simple availability or the possession of basic technical skills. For comprehension to take place, and for what is read to have meaning, the would-be reader must possess a reservoir of experiences and concepts as a background for what is read, and from which to draw images implied by words. The lack of this background and the absence of motivation, or even recognition of the values of reading, constitutes a barrier to access.

Under the principle of access then, we are concerned not only with the provision of reading materials and the inculcation of a wide range of reading skills, but also with the building of an experiential background for reading as well as the promotion of those factors which lead to the desire to read.

We are also aware of the barriers to access erected by those who would interpose social and psychological—and sometimes, through attempts at censorship, even legal—barriers to reading. Attitudes held by others toward reading, and the environmental prohibitions to effective reading, can serve as deterrents to a child's desire to move beyond attainment of basic skills. Peer pressure among children and young people is an important influence upon their behavior. Where reading is considered antisocial or "sissified", suitable only for "teacher's pets" or, among boys, "for girls only", children are often discouraged from becoming known as readers, even if their own preferences might incline them to read. Adults, too, can have a chilling effect on the pursuit of reading by giving subtle reinforcement to children's "reader-image" prejudices, or perhaps more damaging, by never being seen to read themselves. When parents, teachers or other role models seem not to consider reading as an essential of their own existence, children will be discouraged from believing that it has anything of value to offer them either. Conditions conducive to reading—quiet, sufficient light, a comfortable place to lie or sit, as well as an atmosphere of approval and respect for the reader—are often missing from the home and also from the school.

The paramount importance of improved access, in relation to all of the other elements that make possible the development of readers, emerged as a principle under which several of the recommendations could be clustered. As Peggy Sullivan reminds us in her paper: "Someone has said that the greatest single idea that is most typical of our American society, and which has made it great, is access."

RECOMMENDATIONS

6. *Undertake an inventory of reading resources* in the community: Who are the people and what are the programs that encourage reading and provide materials to read? Findings should be widely disseminated and publicized. Which are the bookstores with selections beyond bestsellers? Where are the paperback bookstores or book-racks in drug or stationery stores, bus stations, and schools? How many news stands are there? How many special libraries in museums, courthouses, public agencies, and businesses are there? What are the reading or storytelling programs in parks, neighborhood centers or community centers? How many public library outlets, branches, stations or bookmobiles are there? What are the school library media centers and individual classroom collections? What are the collections of books or special book-related programs in churches, hospitals, senior centers, daycare centers? How many out-of-school or informal tutoring or literacy programs are going on? What are the industry sponsored programs? Who are the book-related individuals: storytellers, authors, poets?

ACTION: This community inventory might be initiated by the local IRA unit, the PTA, or Friends of Libraries group, but the initiating group would want to widen the circle of concern and enlist the help of many other groups and individuals in (1) getting the information, and (2) finding ways to use it effectively for improved access and motivation. Dissemination might focus on the extent of present use, and opportunities for even greater use. A large reading resources map might be posted in a public place, showing locations of collections, program schedules, resource persons and their availability for talks, performances, or one-to-one mentoring. Small replicas of the large map might be handed out in stores, libraries, and agencies.

7. *On the basis of the community reading* resources inventory, a group might pinpoint where people live in the community who do not now have convenient access to reading resources. A plan might be made for plugging gaps where resources are sparse, nonexistent or unusable, and for improving the situation by removing barriers to physical or psychological access in such ways as: changing service hours at the branch library to better suit the neighborhood it serves; placing rotating collections of children's books and materials for family activities and hobbies near the time clock in a local plant for check-out; providing collections of used (expendable) paperbacks in the waiting rooms of agencies where people experience long waits.

ACTION: The PTA, Friends of the Library group, and/or the local IRA council could support the public library director and trustees, and the school board and administrator, in planning and carrying out these improvements, all of which might require extensive contact with and persuasion of community officials and business and agency leadership.

8. *Publicize and provide* a variety of programs about reading in the home and stress the importance of parents as role models. Highlight the importance of the fathers and other male role-models' interest in reading in order to alter the sex role image of books and reading as being appropriate to girls but not to boys; stress the importance of a psychologically comfortable climate in the home, one that is conducive to the free communication of ideas (everybody's—good, bad or indifferent); of having books, magazines, newspapers, and other items to read and discuss; of having regular family times for reading; of adults and older siblings showing and expressing their pleasure in reading; of tying reading to all kinds of family activities such as television viewing, trips, hobbies, experiments, and even family problems; of providing privacy, quiet, and respect for family members who want to read. Encourage neighborhood surveys to find families who own a lot of books and/or subscribe to several magazines and who would be willing to share or swap with other nearby families.

ACTION: PTA leadership, working with other groups,

should be able to initiate newspaper articles, radio and television interviews, and perhaps a speakers' bureau, to help provide programs for organization meetings, church groups, and the like.

9. *Stress the importance of choices,* varied viewpoints, and the freedom to express these different points of view, as well as to examine alternatives. (This is perhaps a less complicated concept than "intellectual freedom," and leads to the same ends). Try to replace any negative actions taking place or contemplated in the community (such as a campaign to remove books from library shelves) with positive ones (such as more access points for books, more planned discussions of values and aspirations in homes and churches). Hold discussions, interviews, and debates to emphasize the fact that there are indeed two sides (at least) to every issue. Perhaps a club or group might be persuaded to adopt titles such as "Choices" or "Freedom to Choose" as a year-long programmatic theme.

ACTION: Public library trustees and other interested groups might spearhead this activity. Open discussion of this subject is the best antidote to the closed minds and the devious, secretive attitudes that often characterize censorship activity.

10. *Be certain that both* the school system and the public library system have in place a written policy concerning the selection, acquisition, and lending rules concerning all books and other materials. Such policies should include criteria and responsibility for selection, and spell out processes for questioning the materials selected for the library or library media center.

ACTION: The public library director and policy-making board, and the library media director for the system, administrators, and board of education should take responsibility for developing such policies without delay if they do not already have them.

11. *Discover and discuss* barriers and deterrents to reading in the community, the school building, and in the home. Factors may include adult illiteracy, non-English-speaking parents, isolation, excessive television viewing (especially by young children of prereading and learning-to-read age); and low expectations by teachers—and sometimes by parents—of children from poor and/or minority neighborhoods. Devise materials and activities

111

for hard-to-reach parents such as workshops to help non-reading parents. Provide training for bilingual siblings in foreign language homes so that they can help younger children; create radio messages assuring foreign language parents that oral language is an important base for reading in any language; conduct interviews with parents in places where they may be found (supermarkets, health-services centers), asking about expectations for children's reading, their view of the school's role, and the kinds of assistance they would like to have from the school in meeting expectations. The latter is good for consciousness-raising as well as for gathering useful information.

ACTION: This type of activity, initiated by school library media specialists and principals, would require substantial assistance from volunteer groups, members of PTA, IRA, Friends, and others.

12. *The state department* of public instruction should examine standards for reading programs to ensure that they include strong motivational elements, family involvement, and reading for enjoyment activity, and are geared to the development of a higher-than-basic level of reading ability. Of special importance is that standards include new and different kinds of evaluations of reading proficiency, including such measures as variety of the books read, the quality of reports and papers researched and written, the art, music, dance, stories, video programs, slides, and filmstrips created and produced in response to literature and the subject areas investigated through it.

ACTION: The chief state school officer should initiate this with those members of his or her consultant staff concerned with reading. Following initiation, the creation of a statewide consortium of agencies and organizations concerned with reading development should be developed to provide inputs for improved standards for instruction, motivation, and evaluation.

13. *The state department* of public instruction (or other state agency responsible for school library media programs) should examine and revise standards for these programs so that they are stated in terms appropriate to their position within the school's *instructional* program, and are not seen as supplemental or support programs. Requirements in terms of professional staff, materials, and facilities should be high enough to enable library media specialists to be full partners in reading develop-

ment with reading and classroom teachers, principals, and parents.

ACTION: The chief state school officer and/or the state librarian, (depending upon individual state governance and responsibility for school library media programs), should initiate this with the state school library consultant staffs, but consideration by members of the state level consortium mentioned above should be elicited.

14. *State consultants or directors* of reading and school library media programs should collaborate to identify within the state (1) effective programs in which parents and home environment are involved in successful efforts to motivate children to read, and (2) models of good community-wide dissemination procedures concerning these programs. The results should then be distributed to school personnel, organizations, and agencies throughout the state.

ACTION: State level consultants/directors of reading and school library media programs will need to take the lead in this, with assistance from school administrators and members of the reading consortium and local IRA units.

15. *State consultants or directors* of reading and school library media programs could jointly develop—with input from others—a compendium of questions most often asked by parents about their childrens' reading, with answers supplied. In addition to their inclusion in state newsletters sent to schools, agencies, PTAs, and other organizations, these frequently asked questions and answers could be presented to newspaper editors, radio and television producers, plant and labor communications editors, for use perhaps as "filler" material, from time to time. Workshops by the consultant team could be based upon discussion of these, and other, questions.

ACTION: State consultants of reading and school library media programs.

III. THE SOCIETY HAS A STAKE IN IMPROVING THE READING ABILITY OF ALL ITS CITIZENS. LITERACY DEVELOPMENT AND THE PROGRAMS THAT MAKE IT POSSIBLE MUST CONTINUE TO BE TREATED AS NATIONAL PRIORITY ISSUES, HOWEVER OR FROM WHATEVER LEVEL OF GOVERNMENT THEY MAY BE FUNDED.

The society as a whole benefits from having its members achieve higher levels of literacy and its by-products of initiative, imagination, and skill in problem-solving and inferential reasoning. Job and career mobility and productivity will increasingly belong to those who can think clearly and who can use information effectively. Education—and reading, often symbolic as one of the chief tools of education—have been recognized as a national concern ever since this country was founded, one in which the society as a whole has a stake. They must be kept on the agenda of priority issues affecting all the people.

Society is diminished and debased by illiteracy, or by literacy which functions at too low a level. The California Youth Authority, as Mrs. Bush noted, has stated that 50 percent of prison inmates are functional illiterates, reading below the sixth-grade level. Florida Judge Charles Phillips is cited as reporting that 80 percent of new criminals passing before his bench would not be there if they had graduated from high school and could read and write.

It has been noted that one result of higher education and career opportunities for minority group members is its impact on parental expectations of children and of the schools: expectations of both have increased. And, in time, these expectations will decrease the dropout rate and the adult literacy problem, and, with them, a spate of resulting economic and social problems.

The importance to the society of developing, now, in today's children, the highest possible level of influential literacy, is underscored by a look at the demographic facts referred to in Palmer's paper. Because of the drop in the birthrate in the 1970s, a comparatively small group of adults a decade or so hence will have to supply the country's productive energy. They will be responsible for running the country, even while supporting an enormously larger population of elderly people, as well as an expanded generation of children. A far greater proportion of these adults than ever before will come from predominantly low income urban populations—the very group who are right

114

now probably getting the least motivation, the fewest books to read and enjoy, the poorest access to positive experiences, and the least creative teaching.

Emphatically, this is *not* the time to banish reading, libraries or any other part of education from the national list of priorities!

RECOMMENDATIONS

16. *Local fact-finding* should be undertaken to dramatize the fact that illiteracy, or a low level of literacy, correlates with a high degree of crime, young people in various kinds of trouble, and with socioeconomic dislocation in the community.

ACTION: The district school administrator should initiate collaboration with juvenile judges, parole officers, family court officials, and others who deal with troubled and unlawful behavior in youth. They should get the facts, make comparisons and correlations with school and reading records, and publicize the findings. A good case could probably be made that more and better attention, and resources, devoted to a family-school partnership for reading could have benefited the community as well as the individual lives of the young people. Perhaps one of the service clubs could take this information and, in concert with an advisory committee of educators, librarians and youth workers, sponsor a plan for improvements.

17. *Stimulate discussions,* offering materials and speakers, for service clubs and businessmen's and women's groups, at which personnel officers, employment agents and employers talk about the level of thinking/reading skills that different kinds of jobs require today, as well as some of the problems they have in finding people who can perform properly in them. Plan other programs in which journalists, community planners, politicians, and other observers of the community discuss the future development of the community, the characteristics of the people who will be needed to run it, and how reading can help to develop those characteristics. Programs of this kind can be adapted to newspaper articles or radio and television programs. The point is to get people in the community to focus and think about these matters.

ACTION: Local units of PTA and IRA could join in initiating such series of programs, providing guidance and involving service and women's clubs, media people, community officials, and chambers of commerce.

18. *Organize a series of programs or articles* for presentation live at meetings, or on radio and television, or in newspapers, that make clear the relationship between the development of higher levels of literacy and continuing adult education, pre-school, library, and teacher training, and volunteer training programs, among others, and also the society's stake in sustaining them as national concerns, however they may be funded.

ACTION: The local units of PTA and IRA could join in initiating this series of programs, with support and assistance from specialists involved in the various programs discussed, along with Friends of Libraries and other groups.

19. *Various organizations* in the community might be asked to analyze their own enlightened self-interests, or their stake in the development of a highly literate society. This analysis could be filtered up to the state level officials of those groups, and widely disseminated to members in other communities.

ACTION: The school district administrator might ask a service club (perhaps the one to which he or she belongs) to initiate the program and encourage its incorporation by other organizations. The public library staff, trustees, and Friends groups, as well as the reading professionals, could also serve as resource people.

20. *Arrange for the state departments* of public instruction to join Minnesota and Tennessee in making parent and overall community expectations of reading a part of their assessment programs in reading. (See Fay paper).

ACTION: The school district administrator might generate discussion of this proposal in state or local meetings of administrators, and then propose (backing) of the idea by their professional association.

IV. ADEQUATE FISCAL SUPPORT FOR TRAINED PROFESSIONAL STAFF
AND MATERIALS TO OPERATE READING AND LIBRARY PROGRAMS IS
ESSENTIAL.

While dollars alone certainly cannot do the job of teaching reading, or instilling the reading habit, it is not possible to provide the necessary resources for programs without assignment to them of regular budget allocations. Funds should be allocated as part of the schools' budget for instructional programs. This public (tax) money should be the base upon which other support is built—such as funds from the private sector for specific projects or materials. A reduction in funds for reading and library programs is in itself a kind of censorship, a limitation of resources for learning, and an indication of its lowered priority.

Remembering that one of the three major detractors of the success of reading instruction (Dr. Fay's paper) was "lack of adequate fiscal support for materials—especially trade books, and for supportive programs—reading specialists, . . ." it is vital that collections of books be kept up-to-date and attractive if children are to be motivated to want to read them. In a climate of economic scarcity, it seems doubly important that resources be widely shared and made as accessible as possible. Several recommendations herein address this point.

Optimum utilization of volunteers and aides is important, but it should be understood that they cannot operate efficiently without the supervision and guidance of professional personnel who are qualified for reading and library media programs respectively.

Finally, the question of direct private sector funding for reading and for library programs—as well as for other school curriculum areas—has been widely discussed and experimented with, and recommendations have been presented concerning this possibility. However, it should be clear that there are dangers in tapping into business and foundation sources, the chief among them being that programs funded in this way might be tailored too narrowly to the goals and interests of the funders, and non-funded items might get lost.

RECOMMENDATIONS

21. *Provision of a continuing* flow of new books and other materials into both school library media centers and public

117

libraries should be assured by a monitoring committee, organized for the purpose of obtaining additional resources if required. It should be made clear that this is not a selection committee, or one with an adversary position, but a *support* committee for administrators and library media specialists.

ACTION: The PTA, local reading council, and Friends of Libraries group should organize this committee and arrange for gifts of money from various sources for new books if budgeted monies are insufficient to meet the needs expressed by teachers, parents, administrators and librarians.

22. *If schools or public libraries* that are receiving a fair share of budgeted public monies for books and programs still have insufficient funds, a commitment could be sought from local industries and organizations for regular contributions of funds. A business might be asked to adopt a particular school and make itself responsible for providing items not possible to obtain within the budget.

ACTION: The school administrator should follow up preliminary arrangements made through the initiative of the PTA, Friends, local reading council, member or members of the board of education or the library board.

23. *Staff and budget* must be allocated for the training and supervision of volunteers, and for the parent training, involvement, and partnership program to ensure that policies come to something more than just words on paper. These programs should be considered a regular part of the planning and budgeting process. This does not mean, however, that funds must necessarily be tax funds. Private contributions should be sought, and providing them for special projects may be the best opportunity for a local business, corporation, or family foundation to become directly involved with school support beyond tax support. Corporations or businesses might be asked to pay for such specific things as a handbook for parents, a family-school newsletter, or other training materials.

ACTION: The school administrator follows up leads and contacts made by members of the citizens support group.

24. *Long-term loans of materials* from other libraries or other agencies or businesses should be arranged, to fill gaps in collections caused by shrunken budgets. An example might be a

collection of materials on gas production or mining from a local company.

ACTION: The school administrator or district library media director could follow up and make final arrangements on leads and contacts made by PTA, Friends, or other members of the support group.

25. *A plan should be explored* for using school library media collections during the summer months through church, community center and parks/recreation programs.

ACTION: The school district administrator and library media director (or head librarian in the schools if there is no director for the district) should meet with youth and recreation directors, ministers, and others with summer programs to see if they can develop satisfactory procedures.

26. *The state superintendent* of schools, state board of education, and members of the education committees of both houses of the legislature should be urged to allocate adequate funds to maintain reading and school library media programs when title programs in these areas are consolidated into block grants and funds are not specifically allocated. They should be urged as well to establish line items in state budgets for these purposes, and to strengthen those that may already exist.

ACTION: This involves building an information and support base, and becomes lobbying when specific authorizations and appropriations are at stake. It should be conducted by statewide concerned organizations, such as PTA, coalition of reading councils, Friends, trustees of public libraries, and state school library media associations.

V. An ongoing program of family-school partnership depends upon high level policy commitment on the part of
the school system.

In the words of state superintendent of public instruction
Verne Duncan, "I believe that educators have been less than
diligent in seeking family involvement in the educational process, and have, in fact, discouraged such involvement in the past.
Parents are not without a major responsibility in this effort, but
as the staff, hired by the public to manage the education system,
it is part of the educator's duty to initiate the formation of a
family-school partnership to improve the effectiveness of the
educational enterprise."

School superintendents must come to believe, if they still
harbor doubts, that involving millions of parents who are not
now involved in the education of their children, and training
them to have active and meaningful input into the education
process—not just act as rubber stamps for educators—is, in the
long run, in their enlightened self-interest. In fact, it may be the
only route to the survival of public education. Administrators
must understand, and help others to understand, that this will
have long term societal benefits, including parental support for
the schools, increased national productivity, and the enhancement of family strength and cohesiveness.

School staff need to bear in mind that parents are more apt
to be interested in participation if they can see it linked very
directly to their own children's achievement in reading. This is
an important planning consideration. Others include the fact
that the perception of personal gain is fundamental in the
motivational process, both in encouraging teachers and parents
to collaborate in motivating children to read; that there are
parents who are already effective as partners with the schools in
learning, and there are those who will never be; and in between
there's a large group who can and will join in if given the proper
conditions, encouragement, and the rationale and assistance for
doing so; that feedback, visible progress, and appreciation/
reward can play an important part in motivating parents as well
as teachers.

Convenient and psychologically comfortable access to the
schools for the parents, and to the parents for the teachers, must
be provided. The message should come across clearly that the
schools belong to the public, and that parents and community

members should not feel, and must not be made to feel, they are intruders when they enter the buildings. If communication can be facilitated and the perceptions of both parents and school people shift so that the job of developing the reading habit is viewed as an important and shared one, and if parents' natural and intense interest in their children can be channelled into creative outlets, a real partnership can develop.

Of course not all parents will become actively involved, but knowing this should not deter the schools from making the effort to involve them. At the least, all parents can be brought into a passive partnership with the schools. Even a single working parent, with little time to spend, can instill a positive attitude about the importance of reading with enjoyment. Schools must begin with what each family has and not worry so much about what it does not have. The program needs to reach a large proportion of the community; only in this way does it achieve real impact, get beyond the idealized pilot phase, and become effective on a large scale.

As to the schools and their readiness to achieve this, Dorothy Rich was quoted in Verne Duncan's paper as having this to say:

"Schools, no matter how understaffed, have the capabilities of reaching out and effecting parent involvement, using easy, inexpensive materials, and without waiting for what probably won't come—organizational change or massive government funding."

RECOMMENDATIONS

27. *The school board* should carefully consider and establish formal policies for the inclusion of parents as regular and necessary participants in the instructional process. Goals and objectives for the partnership at the district level should be formulated with the cooperation, and inputs, of a wide range of parents and other community members, as well as representative staff members.

ACTION: It may be the school administrator at the district level who encourages the board to formulate these policies, and who assists them in doing so. Parent aspirations and expectations could be heard as part of testimony given at several board sessions at which parents and others are invited to present ideas.

28. *Once adopted, policies* must be reflected in the district and individual school program goals, curriculum guides, and actual classroom instruction and assessment.

ACTION: Policies must be clearly communicated to principals and teachers. It is essential that building level staff be involved in the development, not only of district level policies, but of specific goals and objectives for the individual school and classroom levels. Input should come as well from parents and other community members. The district administrator, and specialists on the administration staff—such as the reading consultant and district director of school library media programs—along with building principals, will be responsible for interpreting policies, and for assisting staff to implement them so that the commitment is felt throughout the system, from the board level to the individual classroom, library, and reading lab.

29. *The schools must show evidence* of firm commitment, a sense of direction, and common purpose before involving parents in specific objectives or activities. However, once parents are involved, the schools must be ready to take and use the parents' ideas. Background materials for planning and carrying out collaborative activities should be prepared in draft-form before involving parents. Staff planning at the district level should include discussion of such questions as:

What channels or systems will there be for asking questions about the directions and activities of the home-school partnership? Who will be the responsible staff?

What materials are needed to serve the family-school partnership? Who finds this out? How are such efforts coordinated so that experiences and information can be shared?

What will be the nature and limits of the schools' role? Will they play the funneling and coordinating role between national organizations and parents or local parent organizations?

Are the schools prepared to fund staff and projects? What minimal use of existing staff and resources are required to establish and sustain an on-going family-school partnership for reading?

What new priority expenditure at the state or national level would best contribute to the support of the family-school partnership at the local level, at reasonable cost?

Do school personnel in key positions possess the resources,

the organizational and interpersonal skills, and the level of interest and commitment required to make the partnership work?

Can the kinds of support and materials they need be made available in simple and inexpensive form?

Are there any special steps necessary to coordinate this particular family-school initiative with other programs in the already on-going family-school partnership? Can the special reading emphasis be grafted on to an existing family-school activity?

How ambitious an enterprise are we talking about and how will this be decided?

What will be the balance of centralized versus localized activity?

Are there models to learn from and, if so, where are they? Are there already community-wide partnerships for reading in place within the state whose approach and programs could be disseminated?

ACTION: The district administrator, with key supervisory personnel and representative reading teachers, library media specialists, and parents should tackle these planning and strategy questions when preparing to bring parents and other community members into the program so that there will be some proposals and directions for them to react to, and to improve upon.

30. *Specific roles* should be suggested for classroom teachers, and for all specialists, including those concerned with guidance, reading, and library media services. The way in which time is allocated may need to be modified. Role expectations may also need to be reviewed.

ACTION: Each building principal should work with a group of staff and parents to develop roles and responsibilities for the support of the family-school initiative in terms of the goals and objectives that have been adopted for the building.

31. *Parents should be involved* with teachers and principals in developing valid evaluation criteria and characteristics upon which to base an understanding of what expectations are appropriate for which child. One major basis might be the extent to which family support will be available. This would mean that parents who are anxious to set a high level of literacy expecta-

123

tion for their child must be willing to work at the process themselves.

ACTION: A realistic attempt to define literacy expectations for each child might take the form of a four-way contract between student, parent, teacher, and principal. This process would be initiated by the principal in conjunction with the reading teacher, and would involve the school library media specialist, and a group of parents to spell out general terms and elements in the reading equasion. Individual meetings with parents and their own children would follow.

32. *All available means of communication* between home and school should be established through the use of a wide range of communications tools: meetings, individual mail, telephone, newsletters, radio and television programs, interviews, parents in the school, teachers visiting in the home, programs sponsored by public libraries and other types of agencies, and flyers and tip sheets sent to the home. The content of these communications would include information about reading, the benefits of the family-school partnership, and specifics about what to do and how to do it. Response should be specifically solicited so that timidity or apathy about participation is overcome. Evidence that feedback, requests, and ideas are being acted upon should be offered in subsequent communications.

ACTION: Initially, communications will have to be developed by school staff, with some parent involvement, but the volume of parent or family contribution should increase rapidly and be reflected in the various communications. PTA and other volunteer groups can actively encourage family response to school communications.

33. *In-home involvement* must be stimulated by the school staff. Schools should prepare and supply materials so that parents can help with instruction and motivation. Activities should be phased, with many alternatives and choices offered, to enable families to take whatever part of the responsibility they are ready for and able to carry at a given time.

ACTION: Reading teachers and school library media staffs, with support from principals and other staff specialists, will spearhead preparation of the material on a building or district level, with input from PTA, IRA units, and individual parents.

Activities should range from minimal or passive, to optimal and active.

34. *Workshops in the school* should be provided for parents prior to their working with their children at home. Emphasis should be placed on specific reinforcement and motivational techniques.

ACTION: Principals, reading teachers or classroom teachers, and school library media specialists will develop workshops with input from parents already experienced in the processes.

35. *Surveys of parent perceptions* and attitudes, as well as assessments of student achievement, should be part of the feedback and evaluation of the program. Interviews with parents of children in a grades 3-6 special reading program who had been involved in an extensive parent-involvement program, provided very useful information about parent-child interaction at home (as noted by Leo Fay). This Indianapolis experience featured home-learning packets and a contract concerning home reinforcement of reading.

ACTION: Parent surveys and interviews could be conducted under the supervision of the district's research director and reading consultant, perhaps with the help of volunteers from the PTA and/or reading council.

36. *The state board* of education should be asked to support the superintendent of public instruction in initiating a consortium of state organizations and agencies that would concern itself with the family-school partnership for reading and literacy development at all levels.

ACTION: Implementation could be urged by state associations of administrators, library media specialists, and a coalition of local reading councils and Friends of Libraries groups.

VI. A STRONG FAMILY-SCHOOL PARTNERSHIP FOUNDED UPON MUTUAL TRUST AND RESPECT IS AT THE HEART OF COMMUNITY PARTICIPATION IN AND SUPPORT FOR READING AND LIBRARY DEVELOPMENT PROGRAMS.

The absence of this partnership has many causes, but they really boil down to lack of awareness, both of the crucial importance of family involvement in successful learning, and of the need for higher levels of literacy and the ways in which it is attained. It also reflects the desire for convenience on the part of both the families and of the schools. It is more convenient for the educators to develop and implement programs unilaterally; it is more convenient for the parents and the community at large to let them do this. It is the children, and ultimately the society, that loses out.

Research shows that the home environment can have a strong positive relationship to reading achievement. As administrator Verne Duncan has told us, "Educators and parents must believe that reading skills can be improved through cooperative effort; that this improvement is important enough to warrant the extra effort involved; and that both parents and educators are sincerely interested in cooperating to improve children's reading skills." It is essential that a wide range of participation modes be offered so that parents can find a way to participate which is compatible with their schedules and abilities.

Parents and other family members must understand that school itself is only a part of the education process for their children—the part provided by direct instruction in a structured setting. But education overall is provided by the home, the media, other agencies, and the attitudes and perceptions of the community as a whole, as well as by the school. Parents must serve as the *coordinators* of this entire education process for their children.

Parents need to become aware that they can clarify their own personal values through reading the thoughts and experiences of others; that they can solve problems by reading about what others did in similar situations. Helping their children starts with helping themselves to learn to read, and to do the kind of in-depth reading that allows them to make decisions about who they are, what they want to be, what they believe and why. When reading is perceived to be an integral part of their existence as parent, producer, consumer, citizen, unique person,

126

and continuing learner, reading habits are modeled for children to absorb and make their own.

Parents need to understand that providing a psychologically comfortable climate for thinking, expressing, discussing, and listening is more centrally the task required of them in the reading partnership than is time spent in direct reading instruction. It is the experiences, the concepts, the vocabulary, the development of images and imagination that lays the groundwork for reading instruction. It is a positive self-identity, a feeling of mattering, and the perception of his or her potential for influence and leadership that motivates a child to want to read and to enjoy doing it.

RECOMMENDATIONS

37. *Educational programs for parents* can be provided during day or evening hours, at the school, in libraries, community centers, business offices, plants, or churches. These programs need not be specifically geared to training to help children, but rather to creating links between reading, thinking, and successful living for themselves. Critically considering and discussing with others what one can expect to get out of reading, will encourage adults to want to work with their children.

ACTION: PTA, other organizations, the public library, or a business could sponsor these forums, using school personnel as resources. The most effective programs are those run in series because the parents and other adult family members have an opportunity to reflect on their own concerns and experiences between sessions, and to obtain answers to questions they have thought about.

38. *School staffs should* try to identify parents who cannot read themselves and help them to learn so that they may become enthusiastic models for children and help them effectively.

ACTION: Identification will be best initiated by the principal who has sought advice from school social workers, guidance counselors, and reading specialists. Arrangements can perhaps be made for help to be given to adult illiterates by volunteer literacy trainers.

39. *A monthly tip sheet of ideas*, do-able within the means and convenience of most parents, should be provided for each

grade. A flyer describing "things to do this month" not only serves as a reminder, but provides a time-frame. This could constitute a type of minimal vehicle for establishing the family-school collaboration. It could stimulate participation by parents who do not have time to go to meetings or training sessions, especially if the tips were not elaborate, as in: (1) providing an atmosphere of respect for the requirements of someone who is reading; (2) help in how to choose books to read aloud, along with some good choices geared to different interests and developmental levels; (3) some ways to make storytelling effective; (4) letting your children read to you; (5) reading a book aloud in daily installments and discussing it as you go along; and (6) television programs to watch and discuss as a family.

ACTION: School and public library media specialists and reading teachers could prepare this sheet, with parent and volunteer help. As time goes by, examples of creativity by parents can be given—people like to know what other people really achieved so that they can copy or adapt it. Specific instructional materials can be included for individual students or for reading groups by the reading teachers or classroom teachers, including directions for using games and tapes.

40. *A parent corner* or family reading corner can be set up in school and public libraries, with special events for special days and occasions (a birthday, grandmother's story hour, and others.)

ACTION: The public library and Friends group, with PTAs and reading councils could organize this activity, in collaboration with principals, school library media specialists, and reading teachers.

41. *A handbook or short booklet* for parents should be prepared. It should include clear and precise information about the uses of books in the lives of children, i.e., to find constructive solutions to the problems of people and growing up; to widen the view of job and career choices; to provide an exposure to science, the arts, and the life of the spirit. Several different booklets might be prepared which would be appropriate to give to parents as children enter school at different levels.

ACTION: Principals could colloborate in the creation of booklets with school library media specialists, reading teachers, and public librarians.

VII. Maximum participation of the widest possible range of persons and agencies is a fundamental necessity to the development of a reading community.

Once parents, other family members, and the schools have demonstrated a commitment to a partnership for enlarging reading opportunity for children, it is time to take steps to engage the larger community in this enterprise—both as individuals and as organizations. If the recommendations under principles 1 and 2—or at least some of them—have been carried out, people will generally be aware of the social utility of reading and of the highest possible level of literacy for all children. They will need to be continually reminded, too, that a positive community climate is essential if the intentions and efforts of the families and the schools are to be reinforced. The idea that people with no children have a responsibility to lend support and to help create a reading climate will also need to be reiterated.

Commissioner Gordon M. Ambach of the New York State Education Department underscores his theme that parent education is not just for parents by emphasizing a vital role for those "who do not yet, no longer, or never will have children" as part of the whole community's responsibility "for the quality of essential connections among generations, among parents and children." Those in charge of making the rules for the media, for business, for government—whether or not they are parents—have a tremendous influence and impact upon the family-school partnership, and upon the literacy expectations and development of the community. Attitudes, interests, and models are seen in unexpected places and in many contexts by children—including those about reading—and may be picked up casually, but can remain permanently. In addition, helpers are needed in many places—to provide general or specific guidance, in the background or at center stage—for the development of a reading community.

RECOMMENDATIONS

42. *Devise a formal plan* to widen the circle of citizens who are involved in the schools, with special attention to those who have no children in the schools. Start with groups and individuals known to have interests and strengths related to youth and

try to create a network of concern. This might be approached by asking each organization, church, club or agency to appoint one member as an adhoc member of a community council on parent/family/school reinforcement, with initial emphasis on reading and the goal of achieving a higher level of literacy in the community.

ACTION: The PTA might invite a non-parent member from each organization to a meeting to explain the reasons for and importance of the reading development or reading renewal effort, and to explain the PTA's own desire to broaden its services to the community in support of the parent-school partnership. Special membership for non-parents might be a part of the recruitment drive.

43. *Widely disseminate throughout* the community factors that are known to enhance reading motivation and reading instruction:

- Adult models who read and enjoy reading and who will take time to talk with youngsters about ideas
- Convenient access to books, and a time and place to read enjoyably
- Parents, students and a community who react positively to the schools and support them. Newspaper and radio are often mentioned as giving community support but seldom television
- Teachers who like to teach and enjoy teaching
- High expectations for student achievement by parents, the students themselves, and the community
- Active home support, often inspired by parent education, in how to help children and encourage them to learn
- Involvement of non-parent family members—grandparents, siblings, other relatives—with children
- Limitation of television viewing, and more linking of what *is* viewed to other activities which make children think about what they see and hear

ACTION: PTA, public library Friends groups, and the local IRA council might join in implementation and arrange to send speakers and conduct short lunch-hour seminars in companies with many employees—factories, telephone company, insurance company, or other businesses.

44. *Publicize the need* for volunteers who "have a way with

children" and who would like to help to develop family-school reading reinforcement. Offer a variety of volunteer-training workshops, focusing on motivational techniques such as story-telling games, and reading aloud. A list of things for people to do with children might be disseminated to police stations, recreation centers, family service centers, clinics, and in other places where adults have periodic or regular contact with children.

ACTION: the public library might be the center for an exhibit of materials, lists, books and guidance, offering periodic training sessions on reading reinforcement and stimulation. The Friends of Libraries and PTA, in collaboration with school and public library and reading specialists, could organize sessions, and publicize, with help from senior groups, Jaycees, et al.

45. *A special effort* should be made to encourage parents to reach children who are not their own. A "Students With Other Parents" (SWOP) might be instituted in which parents exchange children for reading adventures during one afternoon each week for ten weeks.

ACTION: The PTA could sponsor a SWOP, and get prizes donated to the parent-student teams who have had the most fun and made the most discoveries or progress with reading. Each SWOP team would have an advisor (librarian, reading or class-room teacher, principal).

46. *Television stations especially,* and radio stations as well, could be asked to sponsor short segments about parent SWOP opportunities, training hints for reading reinforcement volunteers, highlight success stories, or interview prize-winning teams.

ACTION: A member of the school board, PTA, library board or businessman could approach the broadcasters—anyone involved in the reading enterprise who has the best contacts.

47. *Much information* about the importance of adult literacy and its relationship to children's reading should be disseminated. Library resources should be provided to support all tutoring, basic literacy, and other adult education programs.

ACTION: Public libraries should be primarily responsible for seeing to it that resources are accessible to support out-of-school literacy and learning programs. School administrators/library media specialists might collaborate with public and school libraries on in-school adult activities.

VIII. Early childhood preschool experiences within the family unit and as part of daycare or other learning/play groups can provide the strongest possible base for later reading development.

Reading competency has increased most among those who have benefited from the past ten years of special title programs, particularly those aimed at preschool and disadvantaged children. There can no longer be any doubt that children who are read to, talked to, told stories and with whom television watching is shared, in the years before entering formal learning, are the ones who have the best chance of developing an influential level of literacy.

RECOMMENDATIONS

48. *Launch a community-wide* program such as "Beginnings for Babies" in which a booklet about early learning techniques for parents is given newborns and to all babies below two years of age, with the cooperation of pediatricians, gynecologists, and early childhood and family services agencies.

ACTION: Friends of Libraries could provide a grant and generative power for this project as they did in Farmington, Connecticut (see bibliography of Suggested Readings).

49. *Workshops and seminars* for the parents of all five-year olds (or three to five year olds if possible) should be offered in the school buildings periodically, taught by regular classroom teachers, about helping the child to learn and get ready for school. These would be followed up with brief, practical one-page flyers sent to the homes for review. These flyers would be the basis for living room seminars for sharing experience.

ACTION: The school district, with the assistance of PTA, reading council, and other volunteers would mount and direct these programs as an on-going program.

50. *In connection with the preschool* parent-education program, the schools should set up a formal articulation and feed-in process to inventory reading preparation background, interests, parent support level, and previous experiences and skills of all preschool children coming into the schools.

ACTION: The school district in collaboration with daycare and other preschool units in the community, will assume responsibility.

51. *An inventory should* be taken of the practices of daycare, homecare, and other preschool agencies concerning development of verbal skills, conceptual and reasoning skills, storytelling, reading aloud, borrowing books to take home, watching television with adult reinforcement, and parent education efforts. Assistance for upgrading the level of learning could be offered from various sources (libraries, schools, volunteers) and better articulation with the school program achieved.

ACTION: Initiation can come from PTA, early childhood association and other volunteers with support and guidance from the school administration and staff.

52. *Organize a group* of preschool stimulators—specialists in music, dance, drama, and art—to advise parent groups in workshops, school personnel, and preschool units on rhythms, chants, patterns, games, and exercises that relate to reading development by developing motor skills, perceptions, and others.

ACTION: The Friends of Libraries or arts groups might take the lead in developing this assistance to parents and preschool agencies.

53. *Workshops should be offered* for groups of caregivers in preschool units to train them in techniques and models in reading development, i.e., storytelling, games, book selection.

ACTION: Childhood education groups could be involved in this with reading and library staff members from community and school taking the lead.

54. *There should be a special seminar* offered for sixth, seventh, and eighth-graders in how to help younger children in their own families or in the neighborhood. Training could include:
- oral language practice, i.e., word games
- criteria for selecting books
- how to watch television with children
- how to read and tell stories

ACTION: This could be initiated by school or public librarians, with support from family living or home-making teachers, counsellors, or reading teachers.

55. *Start a radio* call-in show weekly to provide regular information concerning lists of books and activities, oral reading and television-viewing hints for grandparents and other senior

citizens who would like to help children, as well as to provide guest interviews. The type of show described could be tied into programs at senior centers, AARP meetings, on reading aloud, talking with young children, and visits to preschool and daycare centers.

ACTION: Early childhood associations, area agencies on aging, local reading councils, kindergarden supervisors, public library staffs, or a combination of these, could initiate this project.

56. *A daily cablecast* television program should feature question and answer interactive opportunities for families with young children.

ACTION: Businessmen's associations might arrange this, with assistance from professional early childhood, reading and library specialists and other organizations.

57. *Accreditation for daycare* and other preschool learning programs should include, at the state level, a requirement that specific prereading verbal and conceptual development activities be offered to all children.

ACTION: The PTA, local reading councils, state library media associations and early childhood groups should initiate this process.

IX. PRESERVICE AND CONTINUING EDUCATION FOR TEACHERS, LI-
BRARIANS, AND ADMINISTRATORS MUST BE PROVIDED ON A GREATLY
EXPANDED SCALE IF FULLY EFFECTIVE READING DEVELOPMENT PRO-
GRAMS ARE TO BECOME A REALITY FOR ALL CHILDREN.

Leadership in the family-school partnership for reading
and successful living must come from the professionals, but it
can only come from them if they are given, on an ongoing basis,
the tools of such leadership. Before there can be an active
partnership between teachers and parents, administrators and
families, and schools and communities, the concept must be
concretely developed by the collaborative efforts of principals
and teachers, classroom teachers with library media teachers,
reading teachers with library media teachers and reading teachers with subject supervisors, and all professional staff with
support staff and volunteers. All of them must examine, analyze
and restructure their roles and responsibilities in the partnership for reading development.

For those newly preparing to enter the teaching field, far
greater attention must be given to the status and utility of
reading in society, and to the realization that higher levels of
literacy achievement must continue to be developed through the
higher grade levels and in all subject fields. More than twenty
years ago, Dr. Mary Austin's study of the training of "tomorrow's teachers of reading," published at Harvard as *The Torch-
lighters*, made recommendations concerning the preparation of
teachers to teach reading, many of which have still not been
implemented by the majority of teacher education institutions.
Among them was that "basic reading instruction offered to
prospective elementary teachers be broadened to include content and instructional techniques appropriate for intermediate
and upper grades." The study also recommended that "a course
in basic reading instruction be required of all prospective secondary school teachers," and that "colleges offer a course or in-
service training in reading instruction specifically designed for
principals, supervisors, and cooperating teachers." The importance of individualized reading was stressed, even at a time when
few elementary schools had school library media centers to
make this as practical and possible as it is now.

For the classroom and reading teachers, as well as the
library media teachers and administrators already in the field,
in-service or continuing education offered during released time

for planning and preparation offers the best hope of developing a strong sense of professional partnership and shared responsibility, upon which a partnership with parents, families and community can be realistically be built.

RECOMMENDATIONS

58. *An orientation session,* scheduled before the opening of school, should be devoted specifically to reading. The principal should meet with all teachers—including reading and library media specialists on the staff—to review reading expectation levels in general and outline procedures for feedback and evaluation, parent education, and the utilization and training of volunteers. Preceding individual school building sessions, the school district administrator, with reading and library media directors, should meet with principals to review preliminary goals and objectives, plans for parent and community involvement district-wide, and available assistance from district headquarters.

ACTION: Impetus for this must originate with the administrator of the district level—perhaps at the suggestion of reading or library media director.

59. *Regularly scheduled time* should be provided for reading teachers and library media specialists to plan, organize, develop, and evaluate reading development strategies—such as fifteen minutes daily of individualized instruction, sustained silent reading periods, television reading projects. Parent education and involvement and training of volunteers for service to the entire spectrum of reading development programs from instruction to choosing materials and motivational techniques should also be scheduled.

ACTION: Each principal should make appropriate arrangements in the building, with guidance and support from the district administrator and district staff.

60. *Regularly scheduled meetings* of library media and reading specialists with teachers at each grade level should be held in every school building on a rotating basis so that all teachers meet with specialists at least on a monthly basis. These can take the form of mini-workshops at which specific aspects of reading team collaboration are discussed, such as:

- Dealing effectively with hostile or apathetic parents
- Using reading development to entice parents into the school and classroom in non-threatening situations
- Training for-parent education techniques and involvement
- Training for effective work with volunteers and aides
- Individually prescribed reading development programs
- Evaluation of individually set objectives

ACTION: Principals should initiate and plan for these meetings and often sit in on sessions themselves, bringing in other specialists as needed. Nearby teacher-training institution staff members could be asked to assist with occasional sessions.

61. *Provide periodic in-service* sessions in which professional, paraprofessional, and volunteer staff meet together to examine the whole picture of particular areas of the reading renewal and development program in the community. All school personnel who are in any way part of the reading development team need to have some background in such things as: (1) the role of public and community college librarians who work with adult literacy in such settings as neighborhood centers; (2) adult basic-education courses; (3) industry training programs, and (4) rehabilitation programs, daycare centers, and other out-of-school endeavors. Such topics as adult opportunities to model reading behavior for children and literacy requirements for employment would be other topics. Attendance at such a session should be required, at the least, on a yearly basis.

ACTION: The school district administrator would initiate this, bringing in teaching personnel from the community and district as needed.

62. *All volunteers recruited* to work in the instructional program with students should receive rigorous basic training, not only in methods of instruction/remediation/practice, but also in selection and use of materials and motivational techniques relating to the reading development program. Time should be spent in training on providing some background information about the uses of reading, types of reading, how reading relates to thinking, problem-solving, and the like. Volunteers will generally have more time than many teachers to spend just talking things over with children more casually than is often possible in

the classroom, and it is important that they be prepared to make the most of the opportunities they will have.

ACTION: Principals, reading teachers, and school library media teachers should be centrally involved in volunteer training sessions, regardless of who else has coordinating responsibility for it.

63. *Teacher training institutions* should cooperate more fully with local school districts to provide in-service educational opportunities on-site in schools, working with school and district personnel. They should also maintain better professional contact with graduates, answer questions, suggest solutions to specific problems, make research reports available, and in general be more supportive.

ACTION: State supported institutions should be responsive to overtures and requests from state education officials and groups of administrators, prominent alumnae, and, if necessary, members of the legislature. Private colleges should also be accessible and should be responsive to many of the same groups.

64. *Teacher training institutions,* supported by administrators and reading and library professionals, should be urged to structure new types of courses for reading professionals at the supervisory and specialist level. These are the persons who must combine elements of expertise involving not only instruction in skills, but reinforcement and motivation, selection and use of materials, and parent education and community involvement in the development of lifetime reading habits.

ACTION: The need for such courses and specializations should be discussed and urged upon institutions by administrators, reading professionals, and professional groups, with support as needed from statewide library media groups, parents groups, and others.

65. *The state education agency* should make certain that reading and library specialists at the state level are available for consultation with local schools and districts, to assist district personnel in workshops and other in-service activities, and are not just confined to monitoring title funds. State level leadership by a state consultant reading-library media team can focus district-wide and state-wide attention more effectively on the development of higher-level reading abilities than can either one of them working alone.

138

ACTION: School district administrators must be vocal in demanding and utilizing state consultant help.

66. *The state education agency,* with unions and professional organizations, should be requested to take steps to ensure that no teacher be certified for service, in either elementary or secondary schools, without having completed required courses in the teaching of reading, the motivation of reading enjoyment, the use of books and other library materials in the teaching and practice of reading, and the techniques of teamwork with library media specialists.

ACTION: Administrators will have to initiate this in concert with state educational officials.

X. Learning applications of video and computers should be
thoroughly explored and accepted for use in the reading
development program as powerful tools in the hands of
teachers and students, but technology, with its many by—
products which must be *read* cannot be expected to replace
reading.

Technology makes it more important than ever before that
children gain mastery of the full range of reading skills, from
decoding and word association to critical and inferential thinking. Critical listening and viewing skills will have to be taught
along with reading. Teachers will need a great deal of assistance
in dealing with a rapidly expanding information base, and with
the shift away from using the print media as primary sources of
information *coupled with* the shift toward using them increasingly to integrate, rationalize, and give meaning and utility to
floods of raw data. As never before, technology will make
reading a means of transmuting information into knowledge
and power.

RECOMMENDATIONS

67. *Viewing and listening* skills instruction must be provided
for teachers on an immediate and ongoing basis so that they can
teach them to children. These skills include those of critical
thinking as well as decoding, and as such they will need to be
taught when reading is taught if children are to be equipped
with all the tools they need to assimilate and process information
and to deal with feelings and values.

ACTION: This kind of training should be an immediate
priority for in-service programs and could be provided to teachers by closed-circuit video format in specific locations, before,
during, or after school.

68. *Many more programs* must be produced in video formats
for cable access, showing parents and other family members how
to help their children learn at home, how to watch television
with children while turning it into an active rather than a passive
experience; how to follow up its motivational aspects, and how
to cut down on television viewing for a better balance of activities
by applying selection criteria to programs.

ACTION: Statewide or district-wide explorations should be

made of production facilities and talent for creating community-tailored programs for cablecasting into the home.

69. *More books should* be put on videocassette or disc, and material developed to help classroom teachers and families to motivate interest in follow-up activities.

ACTION: A consortium of library, reading, and other associations might develop a production unit in collaboration with a cable broadcasting company.

70. *Software for microcomputers* must be bought or created by school library media specialists, and teachers should be assisted in producing their own programs to help children to do research, use and extend vocabulary, and create their own images. Library media teachers should work with reading teachers in developing and using programs.

ACTION: Library media teachers in consultation with principals and district personnel, should initiate these activities.

71. *Microcomputers and word processors* can be used in the diagnosis, prescription for, and evaluation of individualized programs of reading development, and take much of the drudgery out of these processes—which will in turn encourage more teachers to perform them.

ACTION: Initiative should come from the district administration.

72. *Reading laboratories,* equipped with all of the technology useful for reading practice toward achievement of higher levels of reading skill, should be accessible on a continuing basis for all students, and not solely for remediation purposes.

ACTION: The principal of each school, with guidance from district directors and administrators, will be the person to act upon this recommendation.

Recommendations for National Action

I. THE LIBRARY OF CONGRESS

The Library of Congress should continue to undergird the services and programs of the Center for the Book by providing staff and operational support, and by reinforcing, in every appropriate way, the Center's efforts to raise funds for programs and projects. The base of private sector support on which the Center depends should be broadened far beyond publishers and other members of the communications industries, for at least two reasons: (1) Practically speaking, there is not enough potential for contributed money from the publishing and allied industry sources to support the work that the Center is capable of doing, and (2) an overbalance of funds from this sector makes it appear that reading is a concern only of those whose business and professional interests are directly connected with it. The Library of Congress should direct every effort toward making the mission of the Center more visible for what it truly is: an effort on behalf of the goal that Albert Camus described in *Resistance, Rebellion and Death* (1963): "The aim of life can only be to increase the sum of freedom and responsibility to be found in every person in the world."

II. THE CENTER FOR THE BOOK

The Center for the Book should provide focused, continuous impetus for the acceptance of the ten principles stated in this report, and the implementation of the seventy-two recommendations addressed to state and local levels appended to them. The role of the Center can be both symbolic and operational in promoting reading as the key to successful living, and in maintaining its importance on the national agenda for social and educational programs. It can do this by:

- Serving as the coordinator and disseminator of information regarding efforts to raise awareness of the true role of reading and its implications for individuals and the society

142

- Scheduling reviews of the progress of this effort at meetings of the executive board and other groups with whom board members and staff meet. Continuous review signifies continuing commitment
- Convening small invitational meetings of organization, government, and business leaders to discuss with them the roles they might be able to play in support of the reading development effort at the national, state, and local level. (See recommendations that follow)
- Arranging such meetings within the next twelve months, with at least six of the following (convening up to perhaps fifteen members of board, staff, and leadership of each organization separately): The National Association of Manufacturers, The United States Chamber of Commerce, business and industry associations, Kiwanis, Zonta, the AFL-CIO, The American Newspaper Association, the Magazine Publishers Association, and more if possible; assorted groups of business people—perhaps from particular industries (auto, steel, coal mining, computer software); a government agency such as the Department of Agriculture, with its large representation in the field (county agents and home demonstrations agents). These one-day briefings would include information on the status of reading, the overall aims of the Center, and specific recommendations for action
- Seeking funds from the business community to: (1) commission publications which would identify particular companies (in partnership with the Center), with some aspect of the national reading effort and the importance of the family-school relationship; (2) mount a national awareness campaign; (3) work intensively with the mass media and, (4) provide consultant assistance to groups seeking to implement the recommendations, and meet with staffs and officers of service, professional and other groups.

III. THE FOUR NATIONAL SPONSORING ASSOCIATIONS

AASA, AASL, IRA, and NPTA should renew and reinforce their commitment to the topic of reading, the school and the family partnership in support of reading development, by placing it at the top of their priority list for attention and action. Leadership should make it clear that an allocation of resources to support widespread understanding, acceptance, and implementation of the principles and recommendations put forth in this report, is to be built in to the professional expectations of the association's membership at every level, by:

- Making a leadership commitment—which includes both elected officers, board, and staff—to stay in contact regarding this subject in order to coordinate all opportunities to further the recommendations. This means that the board will not just assign the follow-up to a committee and let them "run with it" (or not, as the case may be), but will provide continuing backing and concern for the association's important effort
- Appropriating some financial support—however modest—for association activities related to this effort
- Appointing a committee or assigning responsibility to an existing committee for implementing recommendations that relate to each association's goals and local unit capabilities; giving this committee authority to work with existing committees and publications where it is useful to do so; and scheduling regular progress reports to the board
- Disseminating principles and recommendations widely to membership through newsletters and other publications, with specially prepared additional material to encourage action by local units
- Scheduling regular programs about the topic and progress in implementing the recommendations in various states and locations at national and regional meetings of the association, and urging ongoing attention at local meetings
- Preparing special material identifying the reasons for the association's commitment to the overall topic and the principles, relating it and the specific recommendations to the association's goals and other aspects of its program. Members could purchase this material at reasonable cost, for distribution to the public, and the board might wish to consider designing and selling other promotion materials, such as posters, buttons, and bumperstickers—sale of which might help support the effort
- Presenting jointly to Congress and to each of the state

legislatures an affirmation of the ten principles, and the request that national and state agendas reflect understanding and acceptance of them
- Enlisting the interest and cooperation of other educational professional groups in the enterprise, especially the National Association of Elementary School Principals, the National Association of Secondary School Principals, the National School Boards Association, the Association for Supervision and Curriculum Development, the Council of Chief State School Officers, the National Education Association, and others.

IV. THE UNITED STATES DEPARTMENT OF EDUCATION

The U. S. Department of Education should serve as the locus of federal government leadership and commitment to the centrality of reading to successful living, and the priority that must be given to relating the home and school to that effort. It must continue to provide visibility and support action to maintain and exceed the levels of literacy already achieved. Even in a period of severely reduced federal support for education programs, the commitment represented by this leadership, coupled with the largest possible appropriation of federal funds, is crucial if dedicated local and state efforts are to be maintained successfully. The Department should:

- Make certain that rules and regulations concerning the disbursement of Chapter II block grant funds are developed and interpreted in such a way that state and local efforts to support reading programs are endorsed and expected
- Ensure that publications emanating from the Department highlight the importance of family-school partnerships, especially where reading is concerned, and underscore its efforts to provide leadership for reading as a national priority
- Demonstrate, through words and the actions of its leaders within the councils of the Executive Branch, a determined advocacy for a continuing effort to support reading, literacy, and library programs
- Serve as a clearinghouse and source of up-to-date infor-

mation about programs and models relating reading to successful living and the family-school partnership

- Encourage the state education agencies and the local education agencies to devote continuing attention and resources to all aspects of the reading program, especially to efforts to project the importance of and the means toward higher literacy
- Study and discuss the recommendations in this report and advise with the Center for the Book on possibilities for their implementation.

V. EDUCATION COMMISSION OF THE STATES

The ECS should facilitate, in every possible way, the dissemination and discussion of all of the principles and the recommendations in this report—especially those addressed to the state level of government—and plan some follow-up action that would lead to awareness and consideration of implementation, by:

- Education committees of the legislatures
- Educational advisors on the Governors' staffs
- The chief state school officers

VI. THE COUNCIL OF CHIEF STATE SCHOOL OFFICERS

It is clear that the new federalism has placed important authority and responsibility for educational planning at the state level. The chief state school officers will exercise an increasingly major role in the planning and implementation of state and local programs and priorities in education which will decide the shape of the reading effort for the next decade and beyond. It is recommended therefore that the Council of Chief State School Officers:

- Endorse the principles set forth in this report, and resolve to upgrade the reading effort in line with some of the recommendations addressed to the state level of authority and responsibility, including: recommendations # 1, 12, 13, 14, 15, 26, 36, 57, 63, 64, 65 and 66.
- Select at least two of these recommendations for immediate priority action

- Encourage the formation of innovative coalitions among the states for an intensive exchange of ideas, models, and even personnel, in support of the family-school reading program
- Advocate to the leadership of the U.S. Department of Education and other executive agencies that reading remain at the top of the nation's educational priorities agenda, and encourage at least basic federal support for reading and library programs
- Encourage local school boards and committees and school district professional leadership to place higher levels of reading competence on their list of priorities, to study the recommendations, discuss them, and give consideration to those they could most greatly benefit from implementing
- Demonstrate by personal example, and in statements, speeches and publications, that the state's commitment to reading as a key component in educating today's children for tomorrow is as great or greater than ever in terms of the economic growth of the state and the viability of individuals as workers and citizens
- Join with the sponsoring associations (consisting of three professional groups and one citizen-education organization), in initiating discussion with the American Association of Colleges for Teacher Education about raising standards of teacher preparation and continuing education for the teaching of reading.

VII. THE AMERICAN LIBRARY ASSOCIATION

The American Library Association should be expected to play a very special and active role in the publicizing of the principles set forth in this report, and in the implementation of many of the recommendations, through several of its divisions and especially through its Office of Library Outreach Services, which coordinates the association's literacy efforts and relationships with other organizations concerned with literacy. OLOS, working closely with the American Association of School Librarians—which is one of the major sponsoring associations—should:

- Alert the great variety of organizations with which it

maintains ongoing communications to the existence of this report and the principles and recommendations identified

• Work closely with the divisions and related organizations most likely to be concerned with implementation of the recommendations at the local community level: public librarians, children's and young adult librarians, trustees, library administrators and public relations personnel, and—among the library related—the Friends of Libraries U. S. A. in addition to many others.

• Encourage ALA units—especially those with journals such as *Top of the News* and *School Library Media Quarterly,* to publish information and suggest specific involvement of members.

VIII. INTEREST GROUPS AND OTHER ORGANIZATIONS

A wide assortment of interest groups and organizations, ranging from unions to churches and citizen advocacy groups, should be brought to an understanding that they have a significant stake in guaranteeing the positioning of higher literacy and reading programs at the top of the nation's social, economic, and educational agenda. They must realize that the formation of a reading society is not solely the province of teachers and of librarians, and is not solely in the interests of publishers, but is vital to the viability of the country into the twenty-first century.

Spurred by the Center for the Book, which will have to take the initiative, with the help of the four sponsoring associations and especially the NPTA, interest groups, and organizations, should be asked to:

• Identify themselves and their goals with the national reading effort

• Alert their memberships to the top-priority status that their leadership accords this effort, and advise the memberships about state and local involvement possibilities in carrying out the recommendations

• Identify themselves with the reading/family/schools effort in publications and media communications

• Offer direct funding support for local or state programs relating to this effort. Perhaps innovative program suggestions could receive consideration for support from social action funds

- Volunteer direct staff assistance to state and local programs, perhaps in cooperation with professional associations, and urge members to volunteer assistance in programs.

IX. BUSINESS AND INDUSTRY

Agents of enormous influence at the local, state, and national and international levels, the leadership of business and industry can have a powerful impact in support of home and school reading efforts. A high level of literacy is crucial to the operation of a high-technology world, and these institutions must be encouraged to take up the challenge of support for programs for which federal dollars have been reduced.

Business and industry, spurred by initiatives from the Center for the Book, together with the four sponsoring organizations, should:

- Give national focus through their publications, advertising (especially television advertising), to business and industry's concern for high-level literacy skills, and do this both on an individual basis and through their trade associations;
- Corporate giving should be increased in the direction of reading and literacy programs at the local, state and national levels. Support for publications, conferences, and model programs are among good possibilities. For example, the publication of this book was made possible in part by a grant from McGraw Hill, Inc.;
- Corporations may want to consider providing "in-kind" support by loaning staff to work with others on aspects of the family-school reading effort, providing facilities for meetings, publications or graphics;
- Corporations could make their endorsement and commitment clear through staff bulletins and newsletters, and released time for certain activities such as in-plant or office meetings.

These national-level recommendations reflect the sense of the meeting as it relates to national leadership. We are well aware that the organizations and institutions to which they are addressed are already taking many of the actions recommended, but perhaps there are some which can be intensified, and others still to be undertaken. With all of these recommendations, addressed to local agencies and persons, to national organizations, and to state and federal governments, we have not offered a single plan but many possible plans for forging a family-school alliance, a working partnership in support of reading.

Appendix A
Agenda for the Symposium

The Library of Congress
The Center for the Book

READING AND SUCCESSFUL LIVING:
THE FAMILY-SCHOOL PARTNERSHIP

A Symposium Held Under the Auspices of The Center for the Book in the Library of Congress, November 18–19, 1981. Jointly Sponsored by the American Association of School Administrators, the American Association of School Librarians, the International Reading Association, and the National PTA. Co-Chairmen: Virginia H. Mathews of the Shoe String Press, and D. Philip Baker of the Stamford, Connecticut Public Schools

AGENDA

November 18 (Wednesday)

8:00 p.m.   Opening Session.
               James Madison Memorial Building, Assembly Room, 6th Floor
               Introductory Remarks: Carol A. Nemeyer, Associate Librarian for National Programs
               Keynote Address: Robert C. Andringa, Executive Director, Education Commission of the States, Denver, Colorado

9:30 p.m.   Informal reception

November 19 (Thursday)

8:30 a.m.   Coffee. James Madison Memorial Building, Assembly Room, 6th Floor

9:00   Introductory Remarks.

9:15   SESSION I. Perspective of a School Superintendent

151

	Speaker: Verne Duncan, Superintendent of Public Instruction, State Department of Education, Salem, Oregon
	Respondents: Karl A. Plath, Superintendent, Township High School District #113, Highland Park, Illinois
	Mrs. A. T. Leveridge, Jr., President, National PTA
10:30	Break
10:45	SESSION II. Perspective of a Reading Teacher
	Speaker: Leo Fay, Chairman, Language Education Departments, School of Education, Indiana University
	Respondents: Mrs. Virginia Macy, Chairman, Commission on Education, National PTA
	Marilyn Miller, Associate Professor, School of Library Science, University of North Carolina at Chapel Hill
Noon	Break
12:15 p.m.	Luncheon
	West Dining Alcove, James Madison Memorial Building, 6th Floor
	Guest Speaker: Mrs. George Bush
1:30	SESSION III. Perspective of a Parent
	Speaker: Edward L. Palmer, Vice President for Research, Children's Television Workshop, New York
	Respondents: Wilmer S. Cody, Superintendent, Birmingham, Alabama Public Schools
	Lucille C. Thomas, Assistant Director for Elementary Schools, Office of Library, Media, and Telecommunications, New York City Board of Education

	Thomas P. Fitzgerald, Supervisor, Basic Skills, The State Education Department, The University of the State of New York, Albany
2:45	Break
3:00	SESSION IV. Perspective of a Librarian

SESSION IV. Perspective of a Librarian

Speaker: Peggy Sullivan, Dean, College of Professional Studies, Northern Illinois University

Respondents: Jack Cassidy, Professor of Reading, Millersville State College, and President-Elect, International Reading Association

M. Richard Robinson, President and Chief Executive Officer, Scholastic Magazines, Inc.

| 4:15 | Summary and discussion |

Lester Asheim, William Rand Kenan, Jr., Professor of Library Science, The University of North Carolina at Chapel Hill

| 5:00 | Informal reception |

Appendix B
List of Participants

The Library of Congress
The Center for the Book

READING AND SUCCESSFUL LIVING:
THE FAMILY-SCHOOL PARTNERSHIP
Library of Congress, November 18–19, 1981

PARTICIPANTS

Olin L. Adams, Jr., Superintendent of Schools, Carroll County, Maryland

Phylliss J. Adams, Professor of Education, University of Denver

Leo N. Albert, Vice President, Prentice-Hall, Inc.

Robert C. Andringa, Executive Director, Education Commission of the States

Lester Asheim, William Rand Kenan, Jr., Professor of Library Science, The University of North Carolina at Chapel Hill

Grace Baisinger, Past President, The National PTA

D. Philip Baker, Coordinator of Library Media Programs, Stamford Public Schools

Toni C. Bearman, Executive Director, National Commission on Libraries and Information Science

Jennie Bechtold, Supervisor of Reading and Elementary Language Arts, Wood County Schools, Parkersburg, West Virginia

Louisa Biddle, Office of Mrs. George Bush

Roberta Biegel, Montgomery County Public Schools, Maryland

Dorothy Blake, President-Elect, American Association of School Librarians

George B. Brain, Dean, College of Education, Washington State University

John Briggs, President, Holiday House

Charlotte K. Brooks, Past President, National Council of Teachers of English

Dale W. Brown, Supervisor, Library Media Services, Alexandria City Public Schools

Marian H. Brown, Cincinnati, Ohio

Betty Jo Buckingham, President, American Association of School Librarians

Mrs. George Bush, Washington, D.C.

Jack Cassidy, Vice President and President Elect, International Reading Association

William M. Cochrane, Democratic Staff Director, U. S. Senate

Wilmer S. Cody, Superintendent, Birmingham Board of Education, Alabama

Jean Coleman, Director, Office of Library Outreach Services, American Library Association

Eileen D. Cooke, Director, American Library Association, Washington, D.C.

Bernice E. Cullinan, Director, International Reading Association

Sandra Dolnick, President, Friends of Libraries, U. S. A.

Verne A. Duncan, Superintendent of Public Instruction, Oregon State Department of Education

Jean F. Dye, The National PTA

Wanna M. Ernst, Library Media Consultant, Charleston County School District, South Carolina

Leo Fay, Chairman, Language Education Departments, School of Education, Indiana University

Alice E. Fite, Executive Director, American Association of School Librarians

Thomas P. Fitzgerald, Supervisor, Basic Skills, New York State Education Department

Lee Galda, Assistant Professor, Department of Language Education, The University of Georgia

James Godfrey, Principal and Library Supervisor, Rye Country Day School, New York

Robena S. Gore, Special Assistant to the Assistant Secretary for Education Research and Improvement, U. S. Department of Education

Ruth Graves, President, Reading Is Fundamental, Inc.

Agnes M. Griffen, Director, Montgomery County Department of Public Libraries, Maryland

Ella Griffin, formerly U. S. Department of Education and UNESCO

James T. Guines, Associate Superintendent for Instructional Services, District of Columbia Public Schools

Mary W. Hill, Westminster College, New Wilmington, Pennsylvania

Elizabeth Hendryson, Past President, The National PTA

Judith King, School Library Media Specialist, Montgomery Blair High School, Maryland

Margaret M. Koryda, Acting Director of Elementary/Secondary Education, Fairfax County Public Schools

Nancy Larrick, former President, International Reading Association

Mrs. A. T. Leveridge, Jr., President, The National PTA

Virginia Macy, Chairman, Commission on Education, The National PTA

Virginia H. Mathews, Vice President, The Shoe String Press

Marilyn L. Miller, Associate Professor, School of Library Science, The University of North Carolina at Chapel Hill

Edward L. Palmer, Vice President for Research, Children's Television Workshop

Julia R. Palmer, Director, American Reading Council, Ltd.

Robert W. Peebles, Superintendent of Schools, Alexandria, Virginia

Karl A. Plath, Superintendent, Township High School District #113, Highland Park, Illinois

Susan Porter-Rose, Office of Mrs. George Bush

Mary Alice Hedge Reszetar, Associate Director, National Commission on Libraries and Information Science

Mrs. Elliot Richardson, Chairman of the Board, Reading Is Fundamental, Inc.

Richard Robinson, President, Scholastic Inc.

Barbara Rollock, Coordinator, Children's Services, The New York Public Library

Mrs. Charlie Lou Rouse, Library Media Specialist, Stillwater Public Schools, Oklahoma

Paul B. Salmon, Executive Director, American Association of School Administrators

Anne Elise Shafer, Media Specialist, Evanston Township High School, Illinois

Mrs. Paul Simon, III, Washington, D.C.

Carl B. Smith, International Reading Association Committee

William G. Spadey, Director, National Center for the Improvement of Learning, American Association of School Administrators

Ralph C. Staiger, Executive Director, International Reading Association

Elaine Stienkemeyer, First Vice President, The National PTA

Peggy Sullivan, Dean, College of Professional Studies, Northern Illinois University

Lucille C. Thomas, Assistant Director for Elementary Schools, New York City Board of Education

Manya S. Ungar, Vice President for Legislative Activity, The National PTA

Phyllis Van Orden, Professor of Library Science, The Florida State University

Lincoln White, Assistant for Education, Office of the Assistant Secretary for Indian Affairs, U. S. Department of the Interior

Karen Whitney, President, School Library Division, Arizona State Library Association

Lois Winkel, Editor, *The Elementary School Library Collection,* Bro-Dart Foundation

Suggested Readings

(Titles with asterisks here cited in text)

*Arbuthnot, May Hill et al. *Children's Books Too Good to Miss,* 7th ed. revised and enlarged. New York: University Press Book Service (302 University Av, 10025), 1979

Association for Library Service to Children, comp. *Let's Read Together* 4th ed. Chicago: American Library Association, 1981

*Austin, Mary C. *The Torch Lighters: Tomorrow's Teachers of Reading.* Boston: Harvard University Press, 1961.

Baechtold, Marguerite and Eleanor McKinney. *Library Service for Families.* Hamden, CT: Library Professional Publications, 1983.

Bell, T. H. *Your Child's Intellect: A Guide to Home-Based PreSchool Education.* Salt Lake City: Olympus, 1972.

Berg, Leila. *Reading and Loving.* Boston: Routledge and Kegan, 1977.

Bernstein, Joanne. *Books to Help Children Cope with Separation and Loss.* New York: Bowker, 1977.

Butler, Dorothy. *Babies Need Books.* New York: Atheneum, 1982
———. *Cushla and Her Books.* Boston: The Horn Book, 1980

Cazden, Courtney. "Peekaboo as an Instructional Model: Discourse Development at Home and at School." *Papers and Reports on Child Language Development* 17, Stanford University, Department of Linguistics, 1979.

Cleary, Florence Damon. *Blueprints for Better Reading.* New York: H. W. Wilson Co., 1972.

Cole, John Y. ed. *Reading in America, 1978.* Washington, D.C.: The Library of Congress, 1979.

Cullinan, Bernice and M. Jerry Weiss. *Books I Read When I Was Young.* New York: Avon, 1980.

De Salvo, Nancy. *Beginnings for Babies: Infant Information Kit,* including resource lists for use with the child under three years old. Farmington, CT: Farmington Village Library, 1982.

Dreyer, Sharon S. *The Bookfinder - Vol. I: A Guide to Children's*

Literature about the Needs and Problems of Youth, Ages 2-15.
Circle Pines, MN: American Guidance Service, Inc., 1977.
II - Annotations of Books published 1975–78.

Ervin, Jane. *Your Child Can Read and You Can Help: A Book for Parents.* New York: Doubleday, 1979.

Fassler, Joan. *Helping Children Cope: Mastering Stress Through Books and Stories.* New York: Free Press/Macmillan, 1978.

Gardner, John W. *Excellence.* NY: Harper, 1961.

Glazer, Susan M. *Getting Ready to Read: Creating Readers from Birth through Six.* Englewood Cliffs, NJ: Prentice-Hall, 1980.

Gliedman, Jon and William Roth. *The Unexpected Minority.* New York: Harcourt, 1980.

Harber, Jean R. and Jane N. Beatty. *Reading and the Black English-Speaking Child: An Annotated Bibliography.* Newark, DE: International Reading Association, 1978.

Hearne, Betsy. *Choosing Books for Children: A Commonsense Guide.* New York: Delacorte, 1981.

Heath, Shirley Brice. "Literacy in a Media World," *Journal of Communication,* Winter, 1980.

———. "What No Bedtime Story Means: Narrative Skills at Home and School", *Language in Society,* 1982.

International Reading Association. *Micromonograph Series* (seven pamphlets) Newark, DE, n.d.

———. *Parents and Reading: A Resource Bank of Projects that Work.* Newark, DE 1982.

Jensen, Julie M. ed. *Children, Language and Schools: Making Them Compatible,* Vol. 59, No. 6 of *Language Arts* (September). Urbana, IL: National Council of Teachers of English, 1982.

Johnson, Ferne. *Start Early for An Early Start.* Chicago: American Library Association, 1976.

Keniston, Kenneth, and the Carnegie Council on Children. *All Our Children.* New York: Harcourt, 1977.

Kujoth, Jean Spealman. *Reading Interests of Children and Young Adults.* Metuchen, NJ: The Scarecrow Press, 1970.

Lamme, Linda L. et al., eds. *Raising Readers: A Guide to Sharing Literature with Young Children* (NCTE Committee on Literature in the Elementary Language Arts). New York: Walker and Co., 1980.

Larrick, Nancy. *A Parent's Guide to Children's Reading.* 5th ed. New York: Bantam, 1982.

Litwak, Eugene and Henry Meyer. *School, Family and Neighborhood: The Theory and Practice of School–Community Relation-*

ships. New York: Columbia University Press, 1976.

Martin, Betty and Linda Sargent. *The Teacher's Handbook on the School Library Media Center*. Hamden, CT: Library Professional Publications, 1980.

Monson, Dianne. *Developing Active Readers: Ideas for Parents, Teachers, Librarians*. Newark, DE: International Reading Association, 1979.

Ogbu, John U. *Minority Education and Caste: The American System in Cross Cultural Perspective*. New York: Academic Press, 1978.

Paulin, Mary Ann. *Creative Uses of Children's Literature*. Hamden, CT: Library Professional Publications, 1982.

Rubin, Dorothy. *Reading and Learning Power*. New York: Macmillan, 1980.

*Sabine, Gordon and Patricia L. *Books That Made The Difference: What People Told Us*. Hamden, CT: Library Professional Publications, 1983

Smethhurst, Wood. *Teaching Young Children to Read at Home*. New York: McGraw Hill, 1975.

Smith, Carl B. *Parents and Reading*. Newark DE: International Reading Association, 1971.

Smith, Carl B. and Leo Fay. *Getting People to Read: Volunteer Programs that Work*. New York: Delcorte, 1973.

Soderbergh, Ragnhild. *Reading in Early Childhood*. Washington, D. C.: Georgetown University Press, 1977.

Staiger, Ralph C. *Roads to Reading*. Paris: UNESCO, 1979.

Sutherland, Zena. *Children and Books*, 6th ed. Chicago: Scott Foresman, 1981.

Sutherland, Zena C. ed. *The Best in Children's Books: University of Chicago Guide to Children's Literature, 1973–78*. Chicago: University of Chicago Press, 1980.

Taylor, D. *Family Literacy: The Social Context of Learning to Read and Write*. Unpublished doctoral dissertation. New York: Columbia University Teachers College, 1981.

Tinker, Miles A. *Preparing Your Child for Reading*. New York: McGraw Hill, 1976.

Trelease, James. *The Read Aloud Handbook*. New York: Penguin, 1982.

Tway, Eileen, ed. *Reading Ladders for Human Relations*. Washington, D. C.: Amerian Council on Education, 1980.

UNESCO. *Promoting Voluntary Reading for Children and Young People*. Paris: UNESCO, 1980.